HUNGER

BASIC TOPICS IN PHYSIOLOGICAL PSYCHOLOGY SERIES
Robert A. McCleary, Editor

HUNGER
A Biopsychological Analysis
Saul Balagura

HUNGER

A

BIOPSYCHOLOGICAL

ANALYSIS

SAUL BALAGURA

BASIC BOOKS, INC., PUBLISHERS

NEW YORK

I dedicate this book to
my first two teachers
SARA AND ITCO BALAGURA

© 1973 by Basic Books, Inc.
Library of Congress Catalog Card Number: 73-78464
SBN: 465-03190-0
Manufactured in the United States of America
73 74 75 76 77   10 9 8 7 6 5 4 3 2 1

Preface

This book has been written so that professionals from other fields and "intelligent laymen" can understand it. I have attempted to take the reader through a series of logical steps, showing him representative work in the various fields of endeavor currently under study. The book is not meant as an exhaustive review of bibliographical data (at the end of each chapter). Its purpose is to take the reader on a promenade through the intricate paths of the regulatory and control systems for food intake. It is also the intention of the author to further the reader's awareness of the complexity of the biological processes that normally operate in the animal kingdom.

The organism is a plastic conglomerate full of fail-safe and redundant feedback systems. It continually molds itself to the external environment in an attempt to maintain its internal environment at a normal level of flux. Any environmental alterations bring about physiological changes to maintain the internal homeostasis. When physiological responses cannot cope, the organism emits behavioral responses to resolve the situation. The nervous system has developed to the point where environmental changes may bring direct behavioral responses aimed at preserving some functional integrity, saving the animal from physiological and biochemical adaptations. Clearly we have arrived at a point where behavior and physiology can be explained in the same terms—this is biopsychology.

In 1916, Anton Julius Carlson published *The Control of Hunger in Health and Disease* (Chicago: University of Chicago Press), emphasizing the role of the stomach as a contributor to the control of feeding. My book emphasizes the central nervous system in the control of food intake. This transition of emphasis has come about as a result of the work of hundreds of scientists. I humbly thank them; without their efforts this book would have been mere science fiction.

Eating behavior has played a supportive role in the biological-social theater in which the leading players are the instincts of "life preservation" and "sex-species preservation." The study of feeding regulation has not commanded the same amount of print as have death and sex. However, no other behavior could occur if the organism did not regulate its energy balance appropriately. Whereas sexual behavior brings about, as a secondary benefit, preservation of the species, eating behavior results in the preservation of both the individual and the species.

The consequences of satiety and hunger have already begun to be recognized by a world unequally divided between the sated and the starved. In the very few sated societies, overeating and obesity are taking their toll. At the same time, the world has never in its history had so many deaths due to malnutrition and starvation. The real scar is yet to be. Millions of malnourished children are growing today to become the adults of tomorrow. In how many of them has inappropriate nutrition already caused developmental retardation and brain damage?

Terms such as satiety, hunger, appetite, and palatability are used frequently throughout this book. They have been given different meanings by various writers. Ascribing the same terms to rodents, monkeys, and man conflicts with the current behavioristic attitudes prevalent among psychologists. However, for the sake of clarity and simplicity, these concepts will be defined in this book in a universal manner to include both rat and man. *Satiety* corresponds to that state in an organism in which no more food is ingested due to the presence or absence of certain hormones, chemicals, or nutrients, resulting in a lack of desire, drive, or need to eat, or in a desire, drive, or need not to eat. *Hunger* represents that state in an organism in which food would be ingested, if available, either because body nutrients and certain chemicals are depleted or because certain hormones and chemicals are present. *Specific hunger* or *appetite* reflects the tendency of an animal to ingest certain foodstuffs selectively. *Palatability* relates to the response of an organism to a foodstuff based on that foodstuff's smell, taste, texture, temperature, and related conditions.

I wish to thank Mrs. Jean Luther for her efficient editorial work. During the entire writing of this book my students, Marilyn Kanner, Lynn Devenport, Donald Coscina, and Donald Smith provided an exquisite model of a positive feedback system; it was often difficult to decide who among us was the gland and who the target organ. Since the pre-embryonic stages of this book, the late Dr. Robert A. McCleary was a guiding friend who provided intellectual sustenance; his advice was always available, often accepted, and seldom wrong. When I undertook the writing of this book, I was naive as to the difficulties normally associated with authorship. Without the help and support of my wife, Ursula, the load would have been much harder to carry.

SAUL BALAGURA

Amherst, Massachusetts 1973

Contents

HUNGER

CHAPTER 1

Basic Characteristics of Eating Behavior

Food and Energy

Although different species of animals have different ways of ingesting their food, all share a dependence on energy for survival. Without energy, living organisms would be unable to maintain their biological structures, and would die. Since this energy must be actively incorporated into the organism, living systems are endowed with extremely complex mechanisms for the acquisition, transformation, and utilization of energy.

In the biological world, energy is transformed from one form to another in three different stages. These stages of energy transformation also indicate forms of energy incorporation into the living organism. The first stage is photosynthesis, which occurs mainly in plants. Photosynthetic processes permit incorporation of radiant energy from the sun by transforming it into chemical energy, which is then used in building organic compounds. The second stage is that of respiration, in which chemical energy is transformed into other biological forms during oxidative processes. In the third stage, utilization, the energy derived from oxidation is used by the organism to do work. This work can occur at the molecular or intracellular levels or can be more systemic, involving multicellular systems.

In order to maintain life there must be a balance of energy, with energy taken in being at least equal to energy spent. Teleologically speaking, it is to keep this balance that an animal must eat. The chemical energy, already derived from photosynthesis and respiration, is contained in substances called foodstuffs or aliments. Through eating or food intake the aliments are incorporated into the digestive tract.

If an organism's energy expenditure is higher than its energy input, growth rate becomes negative; the organism breaks down its own molecules and actually decreases in body mass. If the balance is positive, either growth rate increases or the excess energy is stored as energy reserves in the form of fat.

Decreasing energy intake by food deprivation has been demonstrated experimentally to result in reduced growth or decreased body weight.[26] On the other hand, excess feeding produces rapid growth and increases body weight.[48, 49] The undernourishment observed in so many countries constitutes a sad living example of negative energy balance and its consequences, while social obesity occurs in some affluent societies as a result of a chronic positive balance of energy.

In the biological sciences, energy is most commonly referred to as "calories." In terms of heat, 1 calorie (cal.) is the amount of energy necessary to raise 1 gram of water 1 degree centigrade. One thousand calories are equal to a kilocalorie (Kcal. or Cal.).

The rate of energy utilization by an animal in a relaxed state is referred to as "basal metabolic rate" (b.m.r.). The b.m.r. may be different among individuals of the same species—e.g., significant changes occur during certain diseases—or may vary as a function of species differences. A man weighing 70 kilograms and having a surface area of 1.73 square meters will use up about 80 Kcal. per hour. To be in balance he must ingest 1,800 Kcal. in a 24-hour period; in contrast, a rat must consume approximately 40 Kcal. in 24 hours. While an average man needs approximately 1.2 Kcal. per kilogram of body weight per hour, a rat needs about 5 Kcal. per kilogram per hour. The basal metabolic activity of the rat is thus higher than that of man.

Foodstuffs are generally assigned to 3 main categories: carbohydrates, proteins, and fats, the caloric values of which are approximately 4, 4, and 9 Kcal. per gram, respectively. The caloric value of a foodstuff depends on such factors as absorption, digestion, and metabolization, and their effectiveness in a given organism. For example, substances like cellulose, a carbohydrate, have a caloric value of zero when consumed by a rat or a man, but a value of 3 or more Kcal. per gram when consumed by a ruminant, such as a cow or a goat.

Instrumental Eating Behavior

The organism's attainment of energy is not passive and automatic. Most animals must move around in order to get their energy input. Unicellular animals, however, are usually surrounded by an environment containing sufficient foodstuff in solution, and simple diffusion constitutes the mechanism by which they obtain their food energy. Some more complex unicellular forms possess specialized structures like vacuoles or citostomas, which serve the purpose of a digestive tract. Still more complex systems, such as *ciliata,* have evolved structures that produce currents in the environment which circulate fresh supplies of food near the entrance of the digestive tract. In simple multicellular organisms, such as *hydra,* the problem of obtaining aliments becomes even more critical, and circulation currents in the environment play a very important role in food ingestion.[47]

As we ascend the phylogenetic scale, the problem of acquisition of food becomes even more complex, involving increased use of the animal's nervous system and brain. As animals grow in size and complexity, they become more independent of the immediate environment. Thus, more complex animals may have to go to distant places in order to find food. A large repertoire of activities is performed during the acquisition of food.

Ethologists have dedicated a great deal of time to the study of animals' behavioral patterns in their natural environment. In general, it is agreed that the movement sequence toward the prey or foodstuff consists of a search, an approach, and, for predators, a capture, and an ingestion of the prey.[33] A hungry cat, for example, first fixes on a prey, then follows, catches, bites or kills, and finally eats it. Predation, however, does not necessarily imply ingestion. A cat, whether it is hungry or not, will catch and kill sequentially up to 12 mice. A hungry cat will eat the prey; a nonhungry cat will only catch and kill.[23, 24]

Any activity performed by an animal which leads to acquisition of food is instrumental in the attainment of such food, and can be considered instrumental eating behavior. Not limiting the concept of instrumental eating behavior to certain phylogenetic levels has a great heuristic value. In this book, therefore, regardless of the species position in the phylogenetic scale, movements resulting in the acquisition of food will be considered as instrumental eating behavior.

There are many ways to demonstrate instrumental eating behavior in the laboratory. The learning and running of a maze by ants,[35] the pulling of a cord by rabbits,[6] the pressing of a lever by rats,[37] and the finding and uncovering of a distant food dish by monkeys,[13] are all examples of instrumental eating behavior responses leading to food reward. Examples of this behavior outside the laboratory are the hunting of prey, the chewing of food, and eating with the help of tableware.

Instrumental eating behavior can be defined in the laboratory by accurately specifying a particular behavioral pattern and calling it instrumental eating behavior if, when performed under prescribed experimental conditions, the response leads to eating. Thus, if the experimenter defines the pushing of a panel as the response that will be followed by food reward, and if the probability that the experimental subject will make such a response increases significantly when the response is followed by food, we say that panel pushing has become an instrumental eating response. By this same definition, chewing is instrumental to eating solid foodstuffs, licking is instrumental to eating liquid food, and the probabilities of chewing or licking are very high when the food is either solid or liquid, respectively.

Models of Periodic Feeding

Natural observations make it clear that, at different times, an animal is either hungry or not hungry, eating or not eating; eating is periodic or cyclic. One of the most interesting questions about the eating cycle concerns whether it begins with eating or with not eating. This question is of monumental importance and it is not possible to answer it at the present time. However, let us examine the possibilities that arise from making the attempt.

If the cycle starts in the *noneating* state, the animal must be activated to eat. For all practical purposes, the minimum requirement for a noneating state is a nervous tissue that has continuous inactivity as its primary characteristic. When a state of food depletion develops, another system becomes active and activates a "feeding system." The feeding system might also be awakened directly when supplied with a low level of nutritive substances.

If, on the other hand, the cycle begins in an *eating* state, there must be provision for the feeding system to be subsequently inactivated or inhibited. Otherwise, an animal would be continuously eating. The presence of certain substances, such as nutrients, could activate an inhibitory system which in turn inhibits an ever active eating system, or these substances might directly inactivate the feeding system.

An ethological model should also be considered. Environmental cues, such as the sight of a foodstuff, would trigger a fixed behavior pattern of eating. Once triggered, eating behavior would stop only when the releasing stimulus (the environmental cue) is gone, or when eating is inhibited by internal satiation cues. Figure 1–1 depicts the operational models for eating described in the preceding paragraphs. As we shall see later, various components of all these models contribute to the total regulation of hunger and satiety.

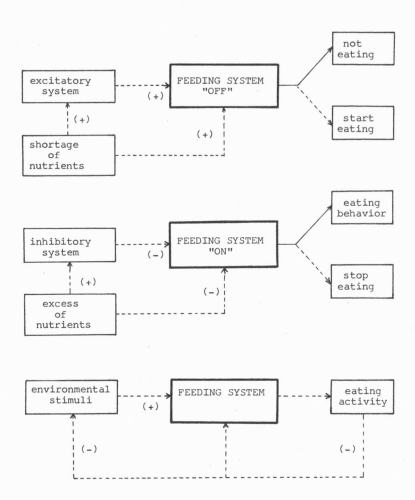

Figure 1-1. The upper part of this figure illustrates the process necessary to initiate eating behavior in an animal that normally has an inactive feeding system: shortage of nutrients directly or indirectly activates (+) the feeding system. The scheme in the middle illustrates a model of an active feeding system in which an excess of nutrients inactivates (−) the normally active tissue, causing an animal that was eating to stop. The bottom portion shows a feeding system that is activated by external environmental cues, such as the sight or smell of food. To achieve normal regulation of food intake an organism must possess a feeding system that combines one or more characteristics of these models.

The Feeding Cycle ·

Study of the feeding cycle must involve consideration of its basic components: meal size, meal length, number of meals, and number of intermeal intervals in a given period, usually 24 hours. No attempt will be made to define a meal in detail; rather, wherever appropriate, the definition used by a specific investigator will be given. One of the concepts on which authors agree is that a meal involves a certain amount of food eaten within a certain amount of time. However, there is disagreement as to how much food should be eaten within how long a time, or what should be the minimal length of the noneating interval between 2 eating periods. As the reader will see, lack of a common definition of what constitutes a meal produces great variability in the interpretation of experimental results.

The speed or density of the emission of eating responses, such as chewing and swallowing, is defined as the ratio between the total amount eaten and the total time spent eating. The number of meals eaten during a given time is an indicator of the frequency of active feeding instances. Another important variable is duration of a meal. Both meal duration and number of meals can be affected by factors such as light and temperature.

The intermeal interval, of course, is an inactive feeding state. The length of intermeal intervals reflects the influence of a variety of physiological satiety stimuli on the organism. It also can be modified externally by light, temperature, and factors inherent in the meal itself, such as concentration and amount of nutrients. The accurate study of feeding needs to take into account all the different components of the normal feeding cycle.

Periodic Eating

Observation of periodic behavior has received great attention, thanks to the pioneering work of Richter.[31] His initial observations were made by means of a cleverly designed environmental cage (see Figure 1–2) which consisted of a living quarter and a small eating compartment. Subsequently, an activity wheel or revolving drum was connected to the living quarter. The compartments were linked to a mechanism that permitted continuous recording of the animal's activity. This setting, or modified versions of it, constitutes the basic experimental equipment currently being used to study such periodic phenomena as motor activity and eating and their relation to such environmental factors as illumination and temperature.

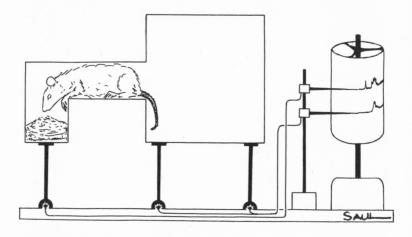

Figure 1–2. An environmental cage used to study eating and locomotor activities in the rat. The living quarter (center) and the feeding compartment (far left) stand on pressure-sensitive devices that activate a recording apparatus (far right) when the animal moves.

In rats, Richter found periods of activity alternating with periods of inactivity, findings which have been observed in many animals, including man. Furthermore, the rats' locomotor activity was greater during the night than during the day; the rat is a nocturnal animal. Since this activity rhythm persisted under conditions of constant illumination, an internal timing device, or biological clock, was postulated in order to account for such periodic behavior independent of environmental factors.[32]

In the great majority of animals, eating behavior occurs periodically [15] and as discrete events. Diurnal animals (e.g., chickens) eat mainly during the daytime and nocturnal animals (e.g., rats) mainly at night. Thus, in a 24-hour period there is a basic 12 hours on, 12 hours off eating rhythm. Rhythms having a 24-hour period are called *circadian,* from the Latin *circa,* meaning "about," and *diem,* meaning "day." This 12-hour on-off rhythm does not mean that an animal eats continuously during the night or during the day, but only that within the 24-hour cycle the animal is more likely to eat during the daytime in diurnal species and during the nighttime in nocturnal species.

When rats are kept in a constant environmental temperature during a 12-hour dark, 12-hour light cycle, the amount of food eaten while it is dark is twice as much as that eaten while it is light. Observations of eating behavior reveal discrete meals, with occasional nibbling. This interspersed nibbling makes it difficult to determine when a meal starts or ends, and an arbitrary definition of a meal must be used. For example, a meal can be defined as the eating of at least 5 food pellets containing 45 milligrams of food per pellet, preceded and followed by an interval of at least 30 minutes. Rats will have about 4 such meals during the day and 8 during the night.[5] Compare these findings with those of Le Magnen,[21] whose rats ate as many meals during the day as during the night, averaging 4 meals during each period. Such discrepancies are accounted for by differences in experimental procedures, such as adaptation time allowed in the test cage or differing criteria used in defining a meal: Le Magnen used a burst of eating preceded and followed by at least 40 minutes. In spite of the fact that these studies report different numbers of meals, they agree that rats eat approximately twice as much during the dark component of the day-night cycle. They have either bigger or more frequent meals during the dark period than during the light period.

Mourning doves are a good example of diurnal animals. Their eating is restricted mainly to the daytime and is characterized by two activity peaks,[34] one at around 10 A.M., the other at 6 P.M., as determined by investigation of the amount of food in the crop. Observations made of some insects of the genus *Drosophila* (e.g., the fruit fly) show that these insects are more active during the daytime, and most of their feeding occurs at this time as well.[28, 42] In man, frequency and distribution of meals depend on age as well as culture. Infants tend to eat periodically every 3 to 4 hours at equally spaced intervals during the dark-light cycle. As they grow and mature, their meals change to a number and distribution determined by learned cultural factors.[22]

At least for the strains of rats thus far studied, eating is not uniformly distributed throughout the dark period.[5, 36] Eating is greater between 8 and 10 P.M. and between 1 and 5 A.M. In addition, it has been observed that more eating takes place during the remaining portion of the dark cycle than takes place during the entire period of light.

The Meal

In 1927 Richter made his classical observations on the eating habits of the rat.[31] He found that rats eat about every 2 to 4 hours and consumed about 10 to 12 separate meals in a 24-hour period. Female rats have a second eating rhythm, superimposed on their basic feeding rhythm, which covers 4 days and is related to the estrus cycle.

In contrast to reports of periodic eating behavior, there is the often-cited study by Baker [2] reporting aperiodic feeding. Rats were placed in an apparatus so designed that in order to obtain food they had to push a panel which exposed a dish containing food pellets each weighing 0.1 grams. A meal was defined as at least 3 panel pushes separated by no more than 5 minutes between pushes. At least 15 minutes had to elapse between 2 groups of responses to constitute 2 separate meals. The records showed no evidence of feeding rhythms, but a closer analysis of the findings reveals that the animals had a mean number of 11 meals per day, that they ate approximately 1.3 grams of food per meal (or 13 pellets), and that the intermeal interval was, on the average, 126 minutes long. The great variability of the data led Baker to conclude that feeding occurred aperiodically.

Other experimenters have shown that, in fact, feeding does occur periodically.[5, 21] However, there are some differences in the observations made so far, as noted in the preceding section. Le Magnen has found that rats eat 61 percent of their 24-hour intake during the night, but the number of meals is the same during the light and the dark periods. Thus, nocturnal meals are bigger than diurnal meals. We have found that rats have approximately 12 meals in a 24-hour period, but these meals are not evenly spaced throughout the whole cycle; the intermeal interval during the daytime is 144 minutes, or twice as long as during the night. These findings are depicted in Figure 1–3.

These studies point toward a discrete meal structure occurring periodically, although not all investigators have been able to

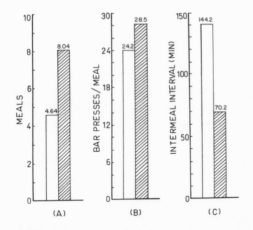

Figure 1–3. Analysis of the meal-eating patterns of normal laboratory rats. Light and shaded bars represent measurements taken during the light and dark periods, respectively. A = number of meals, B = number of bar presses per meal, and C = duration of the intermeal intervals. As can be seen, rats have twice as many meals during the night as during the day, while the pauses between meals are longer during the day than during the evening. From S. Balagura and D. V. Coscina, *Physiol. Behav.* 3 (1968): 641. Used with permission.

demonstrate this with statistical analysis. Baker's conclusion that the rat does not display periodic eating behavior was based on the large variance of the data. From a logical as well as a statistical point of view, the bigger size of the food pellets Baker used meant that fewer pellets were eaten per meal. This reduced the size of the sample and, consequently, increased the variance weight and decreased the probability of obtaining statistical significance.

Modification of Periodic Feeding Behavior

The environment surrounding a laboratory animal is very different from the natural environment. Food can be continuously available to the laboratory animal, while it may not be to the animal in its natural habitat. Even in the natural environment, however, many animals do have a continuous supply of foodstuffs. Protozoa in a pond, for example, have a relatively steady food supply. Similarly, cattle have a continuous supply of grass at least one season of the year. In spite of this, such animals still show periodic eating behavior.

There have been only a few studies of the eating behavior of animals in their normal habitats,[16, 34, 45, 46] and they lack the precision of studies performed under laboratory conditions. However, it is clear, for example, that the eating behavior of carnivores is commonly determined by availability of prey, the time and length of meals and intermeal intervals depending on the size of the prey. Wisconsin timber wolves are known to hunt mostly whitetail deer, but the abundance of other species or the scarcity of deer can increase the incidence of the hunting of other types of prey.[44] A rodent is smaller than a deer and provides a smaller meal, so the wolf will have to hunt more rodents and eat more meals to compensate for the size of the prey. This phenomenon has been demonstrated under experimental conditions in the laboratory, where more manageable species of animals were used.

Even in the laboratory the size of an individual unit of food determines how many units an animal will ingest at a particular meal. For example, the average size of a rat's meal is about 1.3 grams. If rats are trained to perform an instrumental response to obtain either a 0.045 gram or a 0.1 gram food pellet, they will obtain approximately 26 of the former but only 13 of the latter. The size of the unit of food thus determines the frequency of responding until satiation is reached.

Conversely, if the experimenter varies the size of a particular meal, the intermeal interval following it will vary accordingly.[4] When hungry rats are fed by having nutritive material placed directly into their stomachs through a small tube, the time elapsed before they eat a natural meal is dependent on the amount of material initially administered by tube. Hungry rats loaded with 6 milliliters of a liquid diet delay their next meal only 3 minutes; those loaded with 12 milliliters do not have their next meal until approximately 1 hour later.

When the nutritive value of food is altered to contain either more or fewer calories than the rat's normal diet, the rats also change their intake in a systematic way.[1, 12, 19, 43] The nutritive or caloric value of food can be increased by the addition of sugar or oil, or decreased by dilution with a low-calorie material, such as cellulose.[41] It is found that rats compensate for such caloric changes by altering the duration of each meal rather than by changing the number of meals.[12] These findings can be interpreted to mean that, in response to changes in available calories, animals do not alter their pattern of periodic eating—a factor dependent on the clock; instead, they adjust the duration of their meals.

It is well known that locomotor activity, such as running, is highly correlated with feeding activity.[10, 27, 30, 38] Nocturnal animals not only eat more during the dark period but are also more active.[5, 25, 31] Rats, if allowed access to an activity wheel, will run as much as 5 times more during the dark than during the light, up to 10 miles in 1 full 24-hour period!

In many instances, increase in motor activity prior to a meal includes instrumental behavior directed toward getting food. For example, lions in the wild increase their hunting behavior prior to obtaining a meal. A lion in captivity, even though he does not have to hunt to obtain food, increases motor activity, such as pacing, just before the usual feeding time. In other words, there seems to exist some kind of anticipatory motor response prior to the feeding period. This has been demonstrated in the laboratory using other species of animals. If rats are fed once a day for a 2-hour period, and the food is always presented at the same time within the 24-hour period, the activity of the animals will increase just prior to the presentation of food; they become entrained to the feeding period.[8]

In general, the activity periods of a predator are innately determined to coincide with those of the prey. Although this has not been demonstrated experimentally, it could be an example of natural selection. That is, it is possible that those members of a species whose activity cycle is best tuned to their prey may be the most apt to survive.

With respect to feeding behavior, animals show a great deal of adaptation to modifications in the environment. Under ad libitum conditions, a rat does very little feeding between 11 A.M. and 3 P.M., but the animal may completely modify its behavior if food is made available only during this time. This change in behavior does not occur suddenly; it develops with repetition of the treatment.[3] If rats are placed on a 22-hour deprivation schedule [20] (i.e., deprived 22 hours, fed 2 hours every 24 hours) or on a 23-hour deprivation schedule,[14, 29] the amount of food consumed in the period when food is available increases as a function of the repetition of the cycle. These findings indicate that learning plays an adaptive role and can preserve the life of the subject. It is not possible for rats to adapt to deprivation schedules longer than 23 hours in duration since there is a physical limitation to the amount that can be eaten in a certain time period. Adaptive plasticity of periodic feeding behavior has been observed in dogs, cats, man, and many other animals.

Basic Characteristics of Eating Behavior

Animal behavior cannot always accommodate to changes in the environment. If food is presented aperiodically at a time not related to a 24-hour period, the animals' activity will not become bound to the feeding period.[7, 8] For example, rats raised and maintained in 3 different illumination cycles were submitted to a restricted feeding schedule. Food was available through bar pressing at the same relative time within each cycle. The rats also had access to activity wheels in which they could run. It was found that only the animals raised in a 24-hour illumination schedule, and fed at a given periodic time within this period, were able to anticipate feeding time, as measured by increased running just prior to it. Activity was entrained to eating. The animals raised in the 19-hour and 29-hour illumination schedules were not able to anticipate feeding time. In these animals the locomotor as well as the bar-pressing activity was entrained to another powerful environmental stimulus, light. In these latter instances, behavior was not successfully adaptive. Animals living under similar conditions in the wild would have perished.

While it is possible to impose experimentally an abnormal rhythm for certain kinds of circadian periodic behavior, the behavior reverts to the normal 24-hour cycle when experimental conditions permit. For example, squirrels and mice follow a circadian rhythm for locomotor activity when placed on a 12-hour on and 12-hour off schedule of environmental illumination. If lighting is then kept constant, either always on or always off, the animals still show a circadian activity cycle.[11] They continue to be more active during the projected dark period and less active during the projected light period. The mouse can be entrained, for both locomotor activity and food intake, to a noncircadian cycle of up to 8 hours of light and 8 hours of darkness.[18] But if mice are placed back on a 24-hour illumination cycle, or kept in constant light or constant darkness, they will revert to the circadian pattern.[17] This indicates that, while it is possible to override the 24-hour rhythm for certain behavioral patterns, there is a basic inner clock operating on a circadian rhythm.

The Causes of Periodic Behavior

Periodic behavior has been observed in many species of plants as well as in unicellular organisms.[15] In a unicellular system, energy exchange between the cell and its environment operates continuously. The rate of the interaction is probably controlled by the velocity of the biochemical reactions and the diffusion gradients of the system. In other words, the concentration of relevant metabolites determines the direction, rate, and equilibrium point of a physico-chemical process.

In multicellular organisms, all these same mechanisms are operating at the cellular level, but an adaptive interphase develops between the cell and the organism as a whole. That is, the cell in multicellular animals is surrounded and influenced by an internal environment which in turn is surrounded and influenced by the external environment.

The specialization of cell function and the formation of organs can achieve a functional synchronism only when a mediating neuroendocrine system develops. At this stage of complexity, there are several mediating systems between the cell and the whole organism. A molar response can no longer be all or none; rather, it is the product of a summation of individual responses through time. Very often there is no observable response to an external stimulus, an internal response being sufficient to cope with the environmental change.

When a stimulus is presented to the organism, it must first be coded, then carried through the appropriate systems, and finally integrated before a response can occur. The time lag between stimulus and response is also modified by the presence in the organism of a series of intermediate systems such as storage spaces, mechanical transports, metabolic pools, and physico-chemical reactions. These intermediate systems act like buffers between the stimulus and the reactions which follow it, delaying the occurrence of a response (see Figure 1–4). This time delay

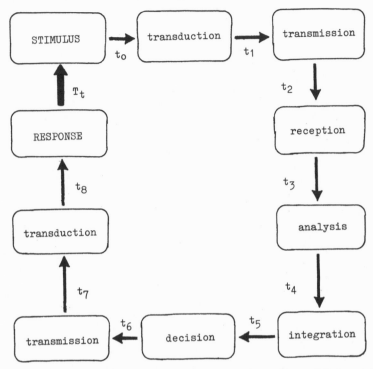

Figure 1–4. The time between the stimulus and the response (T_t) is equal to the sum of the times $(t_0 + t_1 + \ldots + t_8)$ required for the various processes intervening between the stimulus and the response.

is in part the core of periodic behavior and is the basis for the clocklike mechanism built into biological systems.

The stomach was one of the first structures thought to regulate periodic eating. From the work of Cannon and Carlson (see note section for Chapter 6, numbers 29 and 30, page 128) it was known that a series of "stomach hunger contractions" occurred periodically when the stomach was empty. Richter hypothesized that the stomach contractions were synchronous with the loco-motor activity of the animals, and that they were greatly responsible for the periodicity of eating activity.[30, 31]

Richter observed that before they start to eat, rats become active: they walk around the cage, sniff, gnaw, and so on. Locomotor activity comes about 10 times in a 24-hour period; the number of meals in a day is also approximately 10. Furthermore, the stomach hunger contractions occur about 10 times in 24 hours. This led him to conclude that there was a causal relationship among gastric motility, gross motor activity, and eating activity. The periodicity in this cycle was derived from cues originating in the stomach.

We now know that the stomach is not a necessary structure for the regulation of rhythmic activity; animals from which the stomach has been surgically removed also show rhythmic behavior. Eating and gross motor activity may depend to different degrees on autonomic or visceral cues, according to the phylogenetic level of a particular species. Whereas a rat's gastric hunger contractions may correlate highly to its eating behavior, a man's correlation may be very low; in fact, man's eating may depend more on other factors, such as learning and social interaction.

During the last decade, scientists have studied the role of the nervous system in controlling circadian rhythms and periodic activity in general. As early as 1946 Brooks [9] made lesions in the ventromedial nucleus of the hypothalamus of rats, an area of the brain thought to be involved in the regulation of food intake. Prior to surgery, he observed that the rats' eating behavior had the typical cyclical characteristics already described. That is, they ate 70 percent of the food for the total 24-hour period at night, and the intermeal interval was 3 to 4 hours during the day and 1 to 2 hours during the night. Meal size was about 1.5 to 2.0 grams. Lesions of the hypothalamic ventromedial nucleus produced severe alterations of this feeding cycle. The animals' feeding activity increased to 65 percent during the daytime, and they ate regularly every 2 hours irrespective of lighting conditions; the differences in intermeal interval between light and dark periods also disappeared. Meal size increased to 5 grams! But because of historical factors, these findings were not at first interpreted in relation to cyclic behavior.

Richter replicated and expanded Brooks' data. He demonstrated that the circadian feeding activity of the rat disappears when the ventromedial hypothalamus is lesioned by means of an electric current.[32] Richter's lesioned animals, normally nocturnal eaters, shifted their feeding activity so that eating occurred as frequently during the day as during the night, with intermeal intervals shortened to 40 to 60 minutes throughout the 24-hour period. By contrast, he found that removal of the frontal lobes, the septal area, and the pineal body had no effect on the circadian periodicity of eating. Lesions of the lateral hypothalamus also disrupt periodic eating behavior, but this is irrelevant, since this lesion results in cessation of all eating.

Some researchers, such as Strumwasser, have started to study the periodic electrical activity of single brain cells of the sea hare, a primitive salt-water snail that has conveniently large and retrievable neurons.[40] Such cells can be isolated from the influence of neurons in other parts of the nervous system by being removed from the animal and studied while submerged in experimental solutions which keep them alive. Even though they are isolated from the rest of the brain, some of these neurons have a cyclical pattern of activity which remains fairly normal as long as they live in their artificial environment.

Strumwasser has found that these cyclically active cells remain entrained to the light-dark cycle to which the intact sea hare was previously exposed. Studying the synthesis of RNA (ribonucleic acid) and protein in these cells, he has also found that incorporation of protein into the cells depends on the light-dark cycle to which the intact sea hare was exposed prior to the isolation of the neurons. He found a uniform rate of incorporation if the sea hare had been exposed to constant light, but if the sea hare was on a normal circadian cycle of 12 hours of light and 12 of dark, the protein metabolism of the isolated cells reflected this periodicity.[39]

We are still far from solving the enigma of periodic eating behavior, although it has been demonstrated in many species of animals. At present there is no firm understanding of the mechanisms which produce and control periodicity.

BIBLIOGRAPHY

1. Adolph, E. F. Urges to eat and drink in rats. *Amer. J. Physiol.* 151 (1947): 110–125.
2. Baker, R. A. Aperiodic feeding behavior in the albino rat. *J. Comp. Physiol. Psychol.* 46 (1953): 422–426.
3. ———. The effects of repeated deprivation experience on feeding behavior. *J. Comp. Physiol. Psychol.* 48 (1955): 37–42.
4. Balagura, S., and Coscina, D. V. Influence of gastrointestinal loads on meal-eating patterns. *J. Comp. Physiol. Psychol.* 69 (1969): 101–106.
5. ———. Periodicity of food intake in the rat as measured by an operant response. *Physiol. Behav.* 3 (1968): 641–643.
6. Balinska, H. Food intake and type II conditioning in lateral hypothalamic rabbits survived under forced hydration. *Acta Biol. Expt. (Warsaw)* 23 (1963): 115–124.
7. Bolles, R. C., and de Lorge, J. The rat's adjustment to adiurnal feeding cycles. *J. Comp. Physiol. Psychol.* 55 (1962): 760–762.
8. ———, and Stokes, L. W. Rat's anticipation of diurnal and adiurnal feeding. *J. Comp. Physiol. Psychol.* 60 (1965): 290–294.
9. Brooks, C.; Lockwood, R. A.; and Wiggins, M. L. A study of the effect of hypothalamic lesions on the eating habits of the albino rat. *Amer. J. Physiol.* 147 (1946): 735–742.
10. Campbell, B. A.; Teghtsoonian, R.; and Williams, R. A. Activity, weight loss, and survival time of food-deprived rats as a function of age. *J. Comp. Physiol. Psychol.* 54 (1961): 216–219.
11. DeCoursey, P. J. Phase control of activity in a rodent. *Cold Spring Harbor Symp. Quant. Biol.* 25 (1960): 49–55.
12. Epstein, A., and Teitelbaum, P. Regulation of food intake in the absence of taste, smell and other oropharingeal sensations. *J. Comp. Physiol. Psychol.* 55 (1962): 753–759.
13. Finan, J. L. Delayed response with predelay reinforcement in monkeys after removal of the frontal lobes. *Amer. J. Psychol.* 55 (1942): 202–214.
14. Ghent, L. Some effects of deprivation on eating and drinking behavior. *J. Comp. Physiol. Psychol.* 50 (1957): 172–176.
15. Harker, J. E. Diurnal rhythms in the animal kingdom. *Biol. Rev.* 33 (1958): 1–52.
16. Harrington, R. W., and Harrington, S. Food selection among fishes invading a high subtropical salt marsh: from onset of flooding through the progress of a mosquito brood. *Ecology* 42 (1961): 646–666.
17. Johnson, M. S. Effects of continuous light on periodic spontaneous activity of white-footed mice. *J. Exp. Zool.* 82 (1939): 315–328.
18. Kavanau, J. L. Activity patterns in regimes employing artificial time light transitions. *Experientia* 18 (1962): 382–384.
19. Kennedy, G. C. The hypothalamic control of food intake in rats. *Proc. Roy. Soc. (London), B* 137 (1950): 535–548.
20. Lawrence, D. H., and Mason, W. A. Intake and weight adjustments in rats to changes in feeding schedule. *J. Comp. Physiol. Psychol.* 48 (1955): 43–46.

21. Le Magnen, J., and Tallon, S. La periodicite spontanee de la prise d'aliments ad libitum du Rat blanc. *J. Physiol. (Paris)*, 58 (1966): 323–349.

22. Levine, S. Z., and Kowlissar, O. D. World nutrition problems. *Ann. Rev. Medicine* 13 (1962): 41–60.

23. Leyhausen, P. Ueber die Funktion der relativen Stimmungshierarchie. Dargestellt am Beispiel der phylogenetischen und ontogenetischen Entwicklung des Beutefangs von Raubtieren. *Z. Tierpsychol.* 22 (1965): 412–494.

24. ————. Verhaltensstudien an Katzen. *Z. Tierpsychol.* (1956) Beiheft 2.

25. Matthews, S. R. and Finger, F. W. Direct observation of the rat's activity during food deprivation. *Physiol. Behav.* 1 (1966): 85–88.

26. McCance, R. A., and Widdowson, E. M. Nutrition and growth. *Proc. Roy. Soc. (London), B* 156 (1962): 326.

27. Miller, R. S. Activity rhythms in the wood mouse. *Proc. Zool. Soc. (London)*, 125 (1955): 505–519.

28. Mitchell, D. F., and Epling, C. The diurnal periodicity of *Drosophila pseudoobscura* in southern California. *Ecology* 32 (1951): 696.

29. Reid, S. L., and Finger, F. W. The rat's adjustment to 23-hr. food deprivation cycles. *J. Comp. Physiol. Psychol.* 48 (1955): 110–113.

30. Richter, C. P. A behavioristic study of the activity of the rat. *Comp. Psychol. Monograph* 1 (1922): 1–55.

31. ————. Animal behavior and internal drives. *Quart. Rev. Biol.* 2 (1927): 307–343.

32. ————. Sleep and activity: their relation to the 24-hr. clock. In *Sleep and altered states of consciousness,* vol. 45, ed. S. Kety, E. Evarts, and H. Williams, pp. 8–29. Baltimore: Williams & Wilkins, 1967.

33. Ruiter, L. de. Feeding behavior of vertebrates in the natural environment. In *Handbook of physiology,* section 6, vol. 1: Alimentary canal, pp. 97–116. Washington: Amer. Physiol. Soc., 1967.

34. Schmid, W. D. Energy intake of the mourning dove *Zenaidura macroura marginella. Science* 150 (1965): 1171–1172.

35. Schneirla, T. C. Ant learning as a problem in comparative psychology. In *Twentieth century psychology,* ed. P. Harriman, pp. 276–305. New York: Philos. Literary, 1946.

36. Siegel, P. S. Food intake in the rat in relation to the dark-light cycle. *J. Comp. Physiol. Psychol.* 54 (1961): 294–301.

37. Skinner, B. F. *The behavior or organisms: an experimental analysis.* New York: Appleton-Century-Crofts, 1938.

38. Slonaker, J. R. Analysis of daily activity of the albino rat. *Amer. J. Physiol.* 73 (1926): 485–503.

39. Strumwasser, F. Membrane and intracellular mechanism governing endogenous activity in neurons. In *Physiological and biochemical aspects of nervous integration,* ed. F. D. Carlson, pp. 329–341. Englewood Cliffs, N.J.: Prentice-Hall, 1968.

40. ————. Types of information stored in single neurons. In *Invertebrate nervous systems,* ed. C. A. G. Wiersma, pp. 291–319. Chicago: Univ. of Chicago Press, 1967.

41. Taylor, C., and Bruning, J. L. Report of a nonnutritive food substance, palatable to rats. *Behav. Res. Meth. Instrum.* 1 (1968): 32–33.

42. Taylor, S., and Kalmus, H. Down and dusk flight of *Drosophila suboscura Collin. Nature* 174 (1954): 221–222.

43. Teitelbaum, P. Sensory control of hypothalamic hyperphagia. *J. Comp. Physiol. Psychol.* 48 (1955): 156–163.

44. Thompson, D. Q. Travel, range, and food habits of timber wolves in Wisconsin. *J. Mammalogy* 33 (1952): 429–442.

45. Tinberger, L. The natural control of insects in pine woods. I. Factor in influencing the intensity of predation by songbirds. *Arch. Neerl. Zool.* 13 (1960): 265–343.

46. Tugendhat, B. The normal feeding behavior of the 3-spined stickleback. *Behaviour* 15 (1960): 284–318.

47. Ville, C. A. *Biology.* Philadelphia: W. B. Saunders, 1954, pp. 191–198.

48. Wilson, N. L.; Farber, S. M.; Kimbrough, L. D.; and Wilson, R. H. L. The development and perpetuation of obesity: An overview. In *Obesity,* ed. Nancy L. Wilson, pp. 3–12. Philadelphia: F. A. Davis, 1969.

49. Winick, M., and Noble, A. Cellular response with increased feedings in neonatal rats. *J. Nutrition* 91 (1967): 179–182.

SUGGESTED SUPPLEMENTARY READINGS

Harker, J. E. Diurnal rhythms in the animal kingdom. *Biol. Rev.* 33 (1958): 1–52.

Hastings, J. W., and Bode, V. C. Biochemistry of rhythmic systems. *Ann. N. Y. Acad. Sci.* 98 (1962): 876–889.

Mills, J. N. Human circadian rhythms. *Physiol. Rev.* 46 (1966): 128–171.

CHAPTER 2

The Anatomy
of Feeding

The purpose of this chapter is to acquaint the reader with those anatomical structures frequently mentioned throughout the book. Eating behavior is a complex response that involves the whole organism; however, only the anatomy of the nervous and digestive systems will be reviewed here.

The Nervous System

Biologists employ specialized terms to describe the relationships between structures within the body as well as the orientation of a given structure to the body as a whole. To facilitate a description in depth of the nervous system, it is necessary to define some of these terms. There are three major axes, each corresponding to one of three possible dimensions: sagittal, coronal, and horizontal (see Figure 2–1). The sagittal plane divides the body into right and left portions, the midsagittal plane being the middle or median plane. The coronal (or frontal) section is at right angles to the sagittal, dividing the body into anterior (front) and posterior (back) parts. The horizontal plane corresponds to any section at right angles to both the sagittal and coronal planes, dividing the body into upper and lower portions (sometimes into ventral and

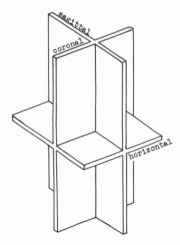

Figure 2–1. The three major planes most frequently used by anatomists when referring to the orientation of an organism or a part of it, e.g., the brain.

dorsal portions). Structures situated closer to the head are termed *cranial,* while those closer to the tail are termed *caudal.* In man and other erect animals, cranial relates to superior and caudal to inferior; in other animals, because of their horizontal position, cranial relates to anterior and caudal to posterior. The word *medial* indicates that a body structure is near the medial plane; the word *lateral* indicates that it is toward the animal's side. Similarly, the word *ventral* refers to the body structure close to the abdominal side; the word *dorsal* refers to the body structure close to the back. A structure near a reference point is called *proximal;* one situated farther away from it is *distal.* Finally, a structure on the same side of the body as a point of reference is termed *ipsilateral,* while one on the opposite side is *contralateral.* Thus, the right arm is ipsilateral to the right leg but contralateral to the left leg.

Traditionally, the vertebrate nervous system has been discussed in terms of its central and peripheral components. The central nervous system (CNS) includes the brain, protected by the skull, and the spinal cord, protected by the vertebral column. The

26

Table 2–1. The main functions of the twelve cranial nerves. These nerves are either motor, sensory, or sensory-motor.

NUMBER	NAME	FUNCTION
I	Olfactory	Olfaction
II	Optic	Vision
III	Oculomotor	Eye Movement
IV	Trochlear	Eye Movement
V	Trigeminal	Mastication; Sensitivity of Face and Tongue
VI	Abducens	Eye Movement
VII	Facial	Taste; Facial Movement
VIII	Auditory	Hearing
IX	Glossopharyngeal	Taste; Swallowing
X	Vagus	Taste; Visceral Function
XI	Spinal accessory	Visceral Function; Neck Movement
XII	Hypoglossal	Tongue Movement

peripheral nervous system encompasses all of the nerves lying outside the central nervous system. This includes the nerves that connect directly to the brain (cranial nerves) or the spinal cord (spinal nerves), as well as nerves indirectly connected to the CNS by way of ganglia, and which supply the skin, smooth muscle, glands, and visceral organs. A total of 12 pairs of cranial nerves are associated with distinguishable sensory and motor functions (see Table 2–1). The spinal nerves enter and leave the spinal cord in an organized fashion at every segment or level of the cord. Their number varies between species; in man there are 31 pairs.

The nervous system is also divided into somatic and autonomic components. Generally speaking, the somatic nervous system governs skeletal voluntary (somatomotor) actions. The autonomic nervous system (ANS) governs visceral responses within the body (visceromotor) and is responsive to internal stimuli (viscerosensory); it is not under *direct* voluntary control. The ANS can be further divided into parasympathetic and sympathetic components.

Anatomically, the ANS outflow differs from the somatomotor outflow in that the bodies of its effector cells lie outside the CNS.

Thus there is usually in the ANS system a synaptic junction between the effector organ and the CNS, with an intermediary ganglion. Neurons proximal to the ganglion are called preganglionic, and they are in direct contact with the CNS. Neurons distal to the ganglion are called postganglionic; they are in contact with a target organ. The parasympathetic system originates from preganglionic neurons in some of the cranial nerve nuclei, as well as from some sacral segments of the spinal cord. The sympathetic system originates from preganglionic neurons in the thoracic and lumbar segments of the spinal cord. The sympathetic and parasympathetic systems tend to function in a highly integrated, complementary way, maintaining a remarkable equilibrium in the internal environment.

The ANS innervates the glands and viscera directly related to some aspect of energy regulation and food intake. Parasympathetic fibers coming from the mandibular and otic ganglia in the head innervate the salivary glands. Fibers coming from the vagus nerve provide innervation to the pharynx, esophagus, stomach, and intestine. Fibers from the pelvic plexus in the lower abdomen innervate the lower intestine and rectum. Activation of the parasympathetic system increases salivation, peristalsis of the digestive tract, and gastric secretion. It is not clear whether parasympathetic activation has a direct effect on hormonal secretions.

Sympathetic fibers coming from the superior cervical ganglion in the neck innervate the salivary glands. Other fibers arising from the celiac plexus in the back of the abdomen innervate abdominal viscera, such as the liver, stomach, and intestine. Sympathetic activation results in increased salivary secretion, inhibition of peristaltic contractions in the intestinal tract, and so on. Furthermore, sympathetic activation also leads to an increase in liver glycogenolysis (which results in an increase of sugar from glycogen).

The ANS also carries sensory information from the abdominal viscera to the brain. Several of these sensory feedback systems are implicated in the regulation of food intake. For instance, information as to the motility or acidity of the stomach is relayed back to the brain via the vagal and celiac systems. The presence of certain chemicals in the liver, such as glucose, results in changes in the neural firing pattern of the vagus nerve. Sensory information carried by the ANS is central to the study of feeding behavior.

The adult CNS is derived from three primitive segments in the embryonic brain: a forebrain, a midbrain, and a hindbrain. As the embryo develops, the forebrain differentiates into a telencephalon and a diencephalon. The midbrain, or mesencephalon, remains as such; the hindbrain develops into a pons, a medulla oblongata, and a cerebellum. Inside the brain there lies a system of cavities or ventricles filled with cerebrospinal fluid.

The top layer of tissue in the telencephalon is called the *neocortex*. Phylogenetic progression upward in vertebrate species is accompanied by proliferation of neocortical tissue. In man and other higher vertebrates (e.g., monkeys, dogs, cats) this proliferation is represented by the presence of large *cerebral hemispheres,* which control the integration of many sensory and motor, as well as intellectual, capacities. The rapid expansion of the neocortex during the evolution of these higher vertebrate forms seems to have proceeded faster than did the enlargement of the skull; the result was turning inward of this tissue to afford greater surface area, producing the wrinkled or *convoluted* outer appearance of the brain. Lower vertebrates, such as rabbits and rats, do not possess these convolutions; they have a smooth or *lysencephalic* cortex. The prominent ridges of cerebral tissue in man and higher vertebrates are termed *gyri,* and the folds between the ridges are termed *sulci.* Some of the more prominent sulci divide the brain into four lobes—frontal, parietal, temporal, and occipital (see Figure 2–2)—whose function is related to higher intellectual processes, as well as complex integration of sensory and motor functions. It should be mentioned that these lobes interplay with each other, and the result has complex effects on behavior and physiology.

Just below the neocortical layer of tissue is a layer of phylogenetically older cortical tissue (*paleocortex*) which has extensive connections with the neocortex as well as with the diencephalic

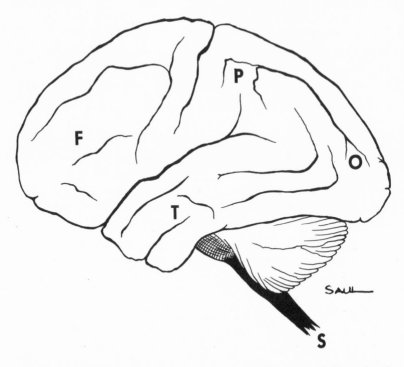

Figure 2–2. Side view of the human brain, showing many of the gyri and sulci that normally occur in animals that possess a developed neocortex. *F* = frontal lobe, *P* = parietal lobe, *T* = temporal lobe, *O* = occipital lobe, *S* = spinal cord.

and midbrain regions. The *striatum,* besides having some motor functions, seems to be important in the control of feeding behavior. Other structures have been described as being the neural substrate of emotionality, since changes in their normal physiology have been associated with marked mood shifts. In fact, this *limbic system,* which forms a belt bordering between the neocortical and diencephalic systems, has been the topic of much clinical and animal research. Among its functions—aside from emotionality—it has been implicated in olfaction and, in some measure, taste processes, both of which are crucial to the expression of feeding behavior.

The diencephalon is covered dorsally by the telencephalon and lies immediately above the base of the skull (see Figure 2–3). Its two main components are the *thalamus,* concerned with such matters as relaying sensory information to other areas of the brain, and the *hypothalamus,* just below the thalamus. Because of its major role in feeding behavior, the hypothalamus demands special attention (see Figure 2–4).

Although relatively small in size, the hypothalamus exerts a major influence on a number of physiological systems. It is well located for this purpose, residing just above the "master gland" (*hypophysis* or *pituitary*), and it is known to exert profound influences over this gland's production and release of hormones. In addition, because the hypothalamus is rich in blood vessels, chemicals reaching the brain by way of the blood stream can substantially influence its neural activity.

Finally, the hypothalamus, located in one of the most important crossways of the brain, is intimately connected with the medial forebrain bundle, a major fiber tract connecting forebrain and midbrain structures. By means of many other pathways, e.g., the fornix, the mamillothalamic tract, the stria medullaris, the stria terminalis, the pallido-fugal tract, the nigro-striatal system, and the dorsal longitudinal fasciculus, the hypothalamus can be influenced and can in turn influence many parts of the brain. From research thus far it seems clear that there is a nuclear region in the basal medial hypothalamus, called the ventromedial nucleus, which exerts inhibitory influences over feeding, and that it is interconnected to an area more lateral to it, the lateral hypothalamus, which facilitates feeding.

In addition to these hypothalamic influences over feeding, to be detailed in Chapter 3, the hypothalamus also mediates water intake, temperature regulation, sexual behavior, and emotional behavior. Moreover, the hypothalamus is important for other physiological processes, such as sleeping and waking.

Two large nuclei are situated at the caudal end of the diencephalon, on either side of the midline and caudal to the hypothalamus; they are called the mammillary bodies. Just caudal and lateral to these nuclei are the cerebral peduncles. These nerve

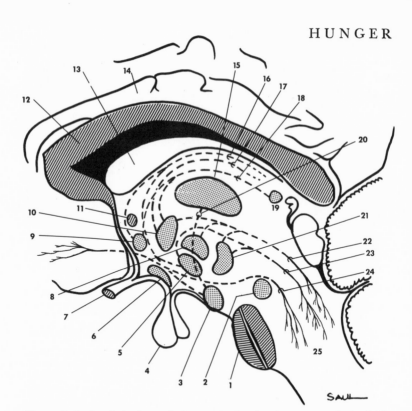

Figure 2–3. Saggital view of the rat brain showing some telencephalic, diencephalic, and midbrain structures. 1 = pons, 2 = red nucleus, 3 = mammillary body, 4 = hypophysis, 5 = ventromedial hypothalamic nucleus, 6 = supraoptic nucleus, 7 = optic chiasm, 8 = dorsomedial hypothalamic nucleus, 9 = proptic area, 10 = anterior hypothalamus, 11 = anterior commissure, 12 = corpus callosum, 13 = interventricular septum, 14 = cingulate gyrus, 15 = thalamus, 16 = fornix, 17 = stria terminalis, 18 = stria medullaris, 19 = habenula, 20 = mammillothalamic tract, 21 = posterior hypothalamus, 22 = dorsal longitudinal fasciculus, 23 = hypothalamotegmental tract, 24 = medial forebrain bundle, 25 = midbrain reticular formation.

tracts, which border the diencephalic-mesencephalic boundary, are related to motor functions. On the dorsal surface of the midbrain, at the boundary between the diencephalon and the mesencephalon, is a midline ovoid structure called the pineal body. While its function remains unclear, in lower animal forms it appears to have importance as a light receptor and may be in-

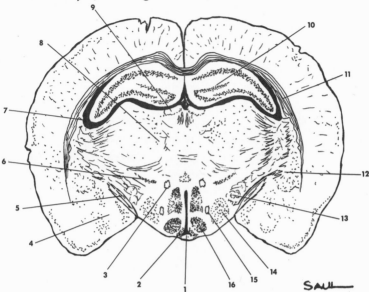

Figure 2–4. A coronal cut of the brain at the level of the ventromedial hypothalamus. 1 = third ventricle, 2 = arcuate nucleus, 3 = mammillothalamic tract, 4 = amygdaloid complex, 5 = optic tract, 6 = zona incerta and fields of Forel, 7 = lateral ventricle, 8 = thalamus, 9 = habenula and stria medullaris, 10 = hippocampus, 11 = corpus callosum, 12 = striatum, 13 = internal capsule, 14 = medial forebrain bundle and lateral hypothalamic area, 15 = fornix, 16 = ventromedial hypothalamic nucleus.

volved in hormonal regulation as well as biological clock mechanisms. More ventrally situated are 2 well-defined nuclear masses, the red nuclei, associated with motor functions. Somewhat more lateral is another nuclear region, the substantia nigra, also involved in motor functions. Its malfunction has recently been associated with Parkinson's disease, which is characterized by tremors and rigidity of the limbs. A complex of cells termed the midbrain reticular formation is arranged in a network fashion around these structures. This complex region has been studied a great deal within the past 40 years, initially because of its significance to the physiological mechanisms which control sleeping and waking. It is now known that this formation also plays an important role in general cerebral arousal, conveying messages up and down the CNS. More recently it has been implicated in the control of feeding.

The midbrain has been studied less with regard to feeding behavior than have the hypothalamic nuclei. However, it is increasingly clear that a major representation of feeding behavior does exist at this lower level of CNS control. The mechanisms are still somewhat uncertain, and localization of function remains to be demonstrated. There is recent documentation that the majority of the brain neurotransmitters, necessary for conveying messages within the nervous system, arise from cell bodies in this region of the CNS.

The Digestive System

Just as some understanding of the anatomy of the nervous system is important when studying the central factors controlling food intake, an understanding of the anatomy of the digestive tract is necessary when studying the peripheral factors which affect feeding. The gastrointestinal (GI) tract is largely similar among mammalian species.

Stated simply, the GI tract is a tube running through the body. Food enters one end and, while being propelled along the tube by muscles in the tube's walls, is broken down both mechanically and chemically so that nutrients within it can be liberated and absorbed into the blood. Once absorbed, these materials are either distributed to the tissues to provide energy and metabolic substrates for immediate utilization by the cells, or stored in different forms (e.g., fat or glycogen) as energy reserves. Constituents which are of no nutritional value or which cannot be processed or absorbed by the GI tract are accumulated and expelled periodically through the other (anal) end of the tube.

A cross section of a segment of gut, as the intestine is also called, allows us to visualize the muscular and glandular structures common to most GI tracts (see Figure 2–5). The outer

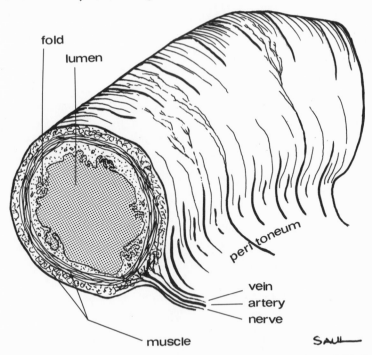

Figure 2–5. A segment of intestine showing a cross section of its wall. Notice the longitudinal and circular layers of muscle as well as the innermost mucosal layer that forms the intestinal folds.

portion of the tube is composed of smooth muscle arranged in two layers: an outer longitudinal layer and an inner circular layer. Contraction of the longitudinal layer shortens the gut; contraction of the circular layer constricts the interior, or lumen, of the tube. The inner surface of the intestine is a mucus-secreting tissue, known as the mucosal layer. The thick mucus secreted here protects the inner lining and also serves as a lubricant to assist movement of food through the lumen. In specialized areas within this layer, reside mucosal glands which secrete digestive juices into the GI tract. The absorptive and secretory surfaces of the intestine are greatly increased by means of foldlike processes that project into the intestinal lumen. There are 2 main types of coordinated muscular movement within the GI tract: (a) propulsive or peristaltic movements, caused by a slow progression of constriction in the circular muscles, and (b) mixing movements, caused either by weak peristalsis that is not sufficient to move food along the gut, or by segmental movements (simultaneous, isolated contractions along several portions of the gut).

For better understanding of the specific structures and mechanisms involved in the processing of food, let us follow a mouthful of food through the GI tract. The first structure encountered is the mouth, where, through chewing or mastication, the mechanical destruction of food begins. At the same time, the food is mixed with a secretion called saliva, which arises from different sets of salivary glands: the submaxillary (under the jaw), the sublingual (under the tongue), and the parotid (close to the external ear). Approximately one-half of all saliva is composed of mucus, to provide lubrication for swallowing; the remaining half is a solution of *ptyalin*. Ptyalin is an enzyme; it initiates the digestion of the starches and carbohydrates in food, a process which is completed in the stomach and small intestine. Salivation is controlled by neurons with cell bodies residing in the superior and inferior salivary nuclei of the brainstem (hindbrain).

Once chewed and mixed with saliva, the food forms a lump, or bolus, which is passed backward along the tongue and into the pharynx. The presence of the bolus stimulates the sensory fibers of the glossopharyngeal and vagal nerves. These stimulated fibers set off efferent discharges through the vagus nerve, eliciting contractions of the esophagus, which connects the mouth with the stomach; the result is the act of swallowing. The food being swallowed is aided down the esophagus by an abundant supply of lubricating mucus. It should be pointed out that only the musculature in the upper part of the pharynx is under voluntary control. Once food passes into the esophagus, a reflexive peristaltic wave is initiated, and the food is carried on to the stomach (see Figure 2–6).

Food in the stomach does not usually go back into the esophagus (except in the case of vomiting). It first resides in the corpus region, the large saclike cavity of the stomach, where, in the first

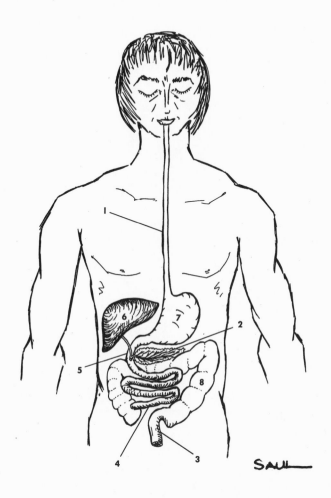

Figure 2–6. The digestive tract and its relative position within man. 1 = esophagus, 2 = pancreas, 3 = rectum, 4 = small intestine, 5 = duodenum, 6 = liver, 7 = stomach, 8 = colon. Many of the substances produced in the liver and pancreas to aid the digestive process are secreted into the small intestine at the level of the duodenum.

of the major digestive processes, digestive juices secreted from mucosal cells act on it. These gastric juices consist mainly of hydrochloric acid and pepsin. Control of their secretion is both neural and hormonal. The neural component is largely mediated

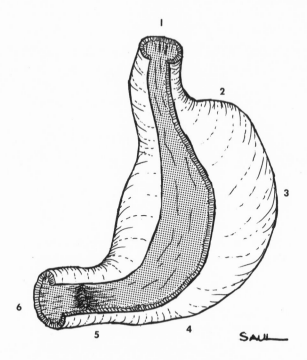

Figure 2–7. The stomach with a longitudinal slit along its wall, permitting visualization of some of the gastric folds as well as the pyloric sphincter. 1 = lower portion of the esophagus and cardia, 2 = fundus, 3 = corpus, 4 = antrum, 5 = pylorus and pyloric sphincter, 6 = duodenum.

by way of the vagus nerve, while the hormonal component occurs when proteins enter the antrum at the distal end of the stomach; *gastrin* is then released into the blood, affecting the release of strongly acidic juices into the stomach. The chemical action of the digestive juices is assisted by frequent tonic, mixing movements which pass along the stomach wall. These gastric contractions eventually move the bolus toward the antrum, where further mixing takes place (see Figure 2–7). When the food has been thoroughly mixed with gastric juices, the resulting solution has a milky appearance and is called *chyme*.

To pass this chyme on to the small intestine, strong peristaltic waves are required. Enough pressure must be built up to push open a normally constricted band of circular muscle called the pyloric sphincter, thus enabling the chyme to enter the small intestine, where it is mixed with a variety of secretions from several organs. The pancreas, a large gland located at the duodenal level, secretes *amylase, trypsin, chymotripsin,* and pancreatic *lipase* into the upper part of the small intestine, and these enzymes contribute to the digestion of carbohydrates, proteins, and fats. The pancreas also secretes sodium bicarbonate to neutralize excess gastric hydrochloric acid. The secretion of these pancreatic enzymes is also mediated both neurally and hormonally. Neural control is by way of the vagus nerve and represents a weak stimulus for pancreatic secretion as compared to the hormonal modulation by *secretin* and *pancreozymin.* The release of these 2 humors from the intestinal mucosa is triggered by the presence of high concentrations of either acid or protein in the chyme. The entrance of food into the small intestine also results in the release from the intestinal wall of another hormone, *enterogastrone,* which inhibits gastric contractions. Some have hypothesized it to be a "satiety" hormone, reducing food intake.

The liver is another organ that provides secretions which aid intestinal digestion. Bile salts, the main constituents of the hepatic secretory solution, assist in dispersing fat globules for easier digestion. Bile is secreted almost constantly by the liver but is stored in the gall bladder, which connects with the duodenum by way of the common bile duct. When fats enter the small intestine, a hormone called *cholecystokinin* is released from the mucosa of the intestine and travels, via the blood, to the gall bladder, where it elicits the gall bladder's contraction and results in expulsion of the bile.

Additional digestive secretions are produced and stored in glands located in the walls of the small intestine itself. These enzymes, which include *sucrase, maltase*, and *lactase,* reduce partially digested carbohydrates to their simplest chemical form. In addition, the small intestine secretes *peptidases* and *lipases* to complete the digestion of proteins and fats, respectively. As do other portions of the GI tract, the small intestine secretes large amounts of mucus for lubricative and protective purposes. Segmental movements of the small intestine mix all these secretions with chyme while, at the same time, peristaltic waves move the mixture along. Both types of contractions are largely of parasympathetic origin.

During the process of mixing and moving the chyme through the intestine, all nutrients and the majority of the enzymes are absorbed by means of specialized structures in the intestinal mucosa called *villi*. The small intestine is emptied in a way similar to gastric emptying. Peristaltic waves build up a strong pressure gradient, generating enough force to push the contents of the small intestine through the ileocecal valve into the large intestine or colon. Once these contents are in the colon, water and electrolytes are absorbed, and the remaining material is propelled forward to be stored in the distal portion of the colon. When sufficient waste accumulates, pressure builds up and stimulates receptors which project to the spinal cord. Reflex firing stimulates the lower colon via the ANS to elicit relaxation of the internal anal sphincter and contraction of the colon sigmoid and rectum. If the external anal sphincter, which is under voluntary control, is relaxed, the mass of waste is expelled out of the body.

SUGGESTED SUPPLEMENTARY READINGS

Crosby, E. C.; Humphrey, T.; and Lauer, W. E. *Correlative anatomy of the nervous system.* New York: MacMillan, 1962.

König, J. F. R., and Klippel, R. A. *The rat brain.* Baltimore: Williams & Wilkins, 1963.

Krieg, W. J. S. The hypothalamus of the albino rat. *J. Comp. Neurol.* 55 (1932): 19–89.

Nauta, W., and Ebbesson, S., eds. *Contemporary research methods in neuroanatomy.* New York: Springer, 1970.

Raisman, G. Neural connections of the hypothalamus. *Brit. Med. Bull.* 22 (1966): 197–201.

CHAPTER 3

Hypothalamic Control

Since 1939 the hypothalamus has been the central focus of experimental exploration of neural structures regulating food intake. Although extensive research has been done since then, developments in the nineteenth century were also of great consequence for the more recent work. Let us consider first the earlier steps that led to present-day scientific trends.

Pierre Flourenz is generally considered to have begun the method of systematic extirpation, or removal, of parts of the brain as a research technique in neurophysiology. He removed parts of the brain from frogs, chickens, pigeons, rabbits, and dogs, and observed resultant changes in behavior. In his famous book *Experimental Investigations of the Functions of the Nervous System in Vertebrates* (Paris: J. B. Bailliere), P. Flourenz in 1842 made what has now become a classic and much quoted observation. Referring to a pigeon from which the cerebral hemispheres had been surgically removed, he wrote:

Once one removes the cerebral lobes, if a movement is begun it will continue; it will never start spontaneously. It will not fly unless one throws it to the air. It will not walk unless it is pushed. It will not consume aliments unless one forces them into its beak. But even more admirable is the fact that the flight, the walk, the ingestion, once commenced, will continue to be performed with an almost perfect regularity (my translation).

If this was not the first observation of experimentally produced anorexia (decreased appetite) or aphagia (not eating at all) in animals, it certainly was highly influential in the development of the field.

From Flourenz's time until the early twentieth century, most research in cerebral mechanisms was performed on the surface of the brain. Lesions were made by removing the skull and cutting into parts of the exposed brain. This early type of research probably resulted from the lack of proper instruments for use in exploring deeper brain structures. In 1908 Horsley and Clark developed the stereotaxic instrument, which provided investigators with the perfect tool for getting inside the brain, penetrating into such structures as the hypothalamus. Discrete lesions in any deep area could be made without damaging any of the more dorsal or superficial structures, thus enabling research dealing with localization of function in deeper brain structures to begin.

The stereotaxic instrument is basically an apparatus that permits the movement of a needle tip in three planes: the vertical, the horizontal, and the antero-posterior. With its help an investigator can calculate the location of a brain structure with respect to a reference point in the skull of an animal. He then sets the stereotaxic instrument to the appropriate reading, lowers the electrode through a predrilled hole in the skull, and automatically reaches the region for which he has aimed. Most of the initial work using the stereotaxic apparatus utilized electricity to produce lesions in the brain, although, more recently, chemical methods have also been used.

Rationale for Lesioning and Stimulation Procedures

The nervous system is organized into (a) afferent or receptive systems that feed information into (b) central or integrative systems that in turn relay information to (c) effector or motor systems which provide the appropriate response. When testing whether a certain neural structure is involved in some type of behavior or function, an attempt is made to interfere with the normal functioning of that structure by incapacitating it, for example, by making a lesion in it. A lesion can be produced by aspirating the tissue,[67] by cutting it,[1] by means of electrical [40] or radio-frequency [70] stimulation, or by using a chemical that will deactivate [28] or damage [83] the tissue. Lesioning a structure that is part of an efferent system leads to deficiencies in the performance of particular motor responses. Results are relatively easy to interpret when the lesion involves the sensory side of the nervous system, rendering the animal unable to detect certain kinds of stimuli. Results are more ambiguous when the lesion is restricted to integrative parts of the brain which serve more complex behavioral functions.

Electrical stimulation is another way of investigating how a neural structure is involved in behavior. For example, stimulation of a motor nerve produces movement in areas innervated by the nerve and therefore demonstrates that the nerve has control of certain groups of muscles. This is also true, although not as clearly, for the central nervous system; stimulation in some areas of the brain can lead to the performance of certain patterns of behavior. Thus, by lesioning or stimulating a brain structure one can demonstrate with reasonable degree of certainty that it is involved in a given behavioral pattern. One must not expect, however, that lesions will always cause a decrease in performance, or that stimulation will always lead to an increase in behavior. A neural structure may normally be involved in the inhibition of a particular behavior, and lesioning it will remove the inhibition. Similarly, stimulation of an inhibitory structure leads to augmentation of inhibition, with a subsequent decrease of behavior.[2, 75]

How is it possible to stimulate a tissue without lesioning it, or vice versa? Sufficient electricity must be produced to cause a significant deviation in either a positive or negative direction in the level of electrical current normally existing in the brain (see Figure 3–1). To produce a lesion, electrical current must be maintained in either polarity for a sufficient period of time. Thirty seconds of a 0.2 milliampere positive current passing through an electrode of 0.2 millimeters diameter will produce a lesion of approximately 1 to 2 millimeters in diameter. To stimulate a tissue electrically without damaging it, the deviation of current passing through the electrode must oscillate rapidly back and forth from positive to negative polarity. A 0.2 milliampere, 0.2 millisecond pulse of alternating current will produce an effective stimulation without lesioning the tissue.

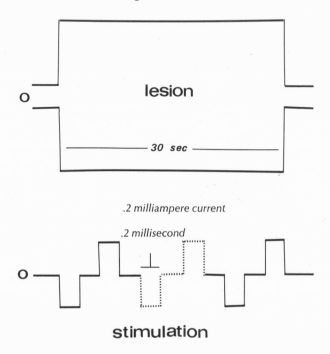

Figure 3–1. Electrolytic lesions are produced by passing unipolar current, either positive or negative, through the tissue (top). The same current level presented in the form of bipolar pulses produces electrical excitation of the tissue without lesioning it (bottom).

Observation of pathological or abnormal conditions has also been important to the development of modern concepts of brain function. Long before man designed methods to produce experimental brain lesions, nature was producing them. Brain tumors are not uncommon, especially those located at the base of the brain, close to the ventral diencephalic area, where the hypo-thalamic region lies. One of the first published descriptions of a case of obesity traceable to a brain tumor was made by B. Mohr in 1840. He described a patient who presented a variety of neurological signs and symptoms, including headaches, visual trouble, dementia, and extreme obesity. After treatment, the au-topsy revealed a tumor of the pituitary gland. Later, in 1900, M. J. Babinski and A. Frohlich reported similar cases. They also believed that the obesity resulted from a lesion of the hypophysis or pituitary gland. The first person on record to disagree with this view was J. Erdheim. In 1904 he reported obesity in patients with tumors located in the base of the brain but not affecting the pituitary. These patients all had in common persistent headaches, a variety of neurological signs and symptoms, and a tremendous desire for food, with consequent overeating and weight gain.

Preliminary experimental evidence in support of Erdheim's contention did not appear until 1921, when Bailey and Bremer reported a case of obesity in a dog resulting from a surgical le-sion restricted to the dog's hypothalamus.[9] The classical experi-ments reported by Hetherington and Ranson in 1939 became most important in further detailing the influence of the hypo-thalamic region in the control of food intake.[40] These investiga-tors produced lesions in the ventromedial hypothalamus of rats, with the help of a modified version of the Horseley-Clark stereo-taxic instrument, and their animals became obese.

Localization of Function within the Hypothalamus

Many workers have now confirmed that ventromedial hypotha-lamic lesions lead to the development of obesity.[18, 41, 42] It is not clear whether this obesity is produced by an increase in food intake (*hyperphagia*) or by a change in the metabolic proc-esses of the affected organism, resulting in an exaggerated storage of energy in the form of fat.[18,20,21,82] Brobeck showed that ventromedial hypothalamic lesions are followed by an increase in food intake, and this stood for some time as the only explanation for the overweight of ventromedially lesioned animals.[17,19] Recent experiments have indicated the existence of metabolic changes—changes resulting directly from ventromedial lesions—that may lead to obesity.[36,37] Thus it now seems that destruction of the ventromedial hypothalamus leads to obesity, not only because of increased food intake but also because of changes in energy balance and fat metabolism.

It is usually assumed that when destruction of a center leads to an increase of a certain behavior, stimulation of that area should produce an opposite effect. Accordingly, one would expect that stimulation of the ventromedial hypothalamic area would inhibit eating behavior and food consumption. The truth of this assumption has been demonstrated and reported for several species of animals.[7,35] Electrical stimulation of the ventromedial hypothalamus does produce both a decrease of food intake and a suppression of food-motivated behavior.[52,90]

In 1943 Brügger reported that electrical stimulation of an area lateral to the ventromedial nucleus between the fornix and the internal capsule led to voracious eating in cats.[23] The hyperphagia was restricted to the period of electrical stimulation (stimulus-bound eating), although in many cases it continued for up to 20 minutes after the stimulation had ended. At the time this finding did not generate much research, and the field remained stationary until 1951, when Anand and Brobeck demonstrated that small lesions of the lateral hypothalamus would cause an animal to stop eating (aphagia) and drinking (adipsia) completely.[2,3] Even if food was presented to it, an animal with lateral lesions starved to death. The aphagia that follows lateral hypothalamic lesions may reflect a breakdown in the neural control of feeding behavior,[75] or may be secondary to a lowering of a set-point for regulation of body weight [69]—the animal would fast in order to bring its weight into balance with the new level of regulation.

In summary: (a) destruction of the ventromedial hypothalamic nuclei results in hyperphagia; (b) stimulation of the ventro-medial hypothalamus leads to aphagia; (c) lesioning of the lateral hypothalamus renders an animal aphagic; and (d) lateral stimulation results in hyperphagia.

Electrical stimulation of the lateral hypothalamus, in the region of the medial forebrain bundle, produces eating behavior in the fish,[33] rat,[3] cat,[4] goat,[53] dove,[38] and monkey.[73] This behavior may or may not be bound to the time parameters of the stimulation. In some cases it starts a few seconds after the beginning of the stimulation and ends when the stimulation ends or immediately thereafter.[10] In other cases there is a sustained effect in which eating occurs even though stimulation has terminated; there are instances in which eating has continued from 40 to 70 hours after the initial stimulation has subsided.[26, 74] An animal stimulated in the lateral hypothalamus will not only eat food which is lying freely on the floor but will actually perform an operant response, e.g., press a lever, in order to get food.[25] The behavior caused by lateral hypothalamic stimulation thus resembles the behavior caused by normal hunger.

In the absence of food, stimulation of the lateral hypothalamic area sometimes produces drinking, i.e., stimulation-bound drinking behavior.[62] In some animals stimulation of the lateral hypothalamus in the presence of water will lead to drinking even if food is available. The behavior produced by the stimulation, be it drinking or eating, may or may not be specific to a single neural system. It is possible to change an animal, originally a stimulation-bound eater, into a stimulation-bound drinker, or vice versa.[84, 88] For example, if a stimulation-bound eater is placed in a cage with water but without food, and is brain stimulated overnight, stimulation of the brain on the following day may result in stimulation-bound drinking rather than eating. It appears that this is a modifiable neurophysiological system rather than a fixed one.

Interaction of the Lateral and the
Ventromedial Hypothalamus

In order for a normal eating pattern to occur, a balanced relationship must exist not only between the lateral and the ventromedial nuclei on one side of the brain, but between each of these areas on both sides of the hypothalamus. Only bilateral destruction of the ventromedial nuclei, for example, will produce a clearcut case of hyperphagia. When only 1 of the 2 nuclei is destroyed, a transient and rather small hyperphagia develops.[2] Similarly, destruction of only 1 lateral area results in hypophagia with anorexia,[31] rather than full aphagia. In order to obtain total reduction of food intake, one must perform a bilateral lesion.

Furthermore, the medial and lateral areas seem to be interacting continuously, so the question arises as to whether they are both acting upon a third structure or upon each other. Experimental findings originally suggested that the ventromedial hypothalamus acts on the lateral to produce inhibition of food intake, the presence of the lateral hypothalamus being necessary for the ventromedial nucleus to exert its inhibitory function. As we have seen, if one destroys the ventromedial hypothalamus, leaving intact the lateral, an animal becomes hyperphagic. Another way of demonstrating this principle is to first render an animal aphagic by destroying the lateral hypothalamus; after that, destruction of the ventromedial nuclei fails to produce hyperphagia.[2, 3] Modern theory espouses a mutual relationship between these centers, such that the ventromedial area exerts influence on the lateral at the same time that the lateral exerts influence on the ventromedial. This type of functional relationship is indicated by studies in which the electrical activity of these regions was studied under conditions of both satiety and deprivation.

Normally, both hypothalamic centers remain active (baseline neural activity), but in starved animals lateral neural activity is found to be higher than ventromedial activity. In sated animals, or during glucose injections, the ventromedial hypothalamus is found to be more active than the lateral. Such shifts in electrical activity correlate well with changes in rate of utilization of glucose by peripheral tissues, as measured by the difference between arterial and venous glucose.[5, 6] Moreover, there exists a reciprocity of action or a mutual inhibition between these two centers: [64, 65, 66] if ventromedial activity increases, lateral activity decreases, and vice versa. The anatomical substrates for such neural interrelations were mapped quite recently. Originally, only connections from the lateral to the ventromedial hypothalami had been demonstrated to exist, but late in 1966 connections from the ventromedial to the lateral hypothalami were also anatomically demonstrated,[8] and the gap that had existed in the correlation between neurophysiological and anatomical findings was closed.

Recovery of Eating Regulation Following Brain Lesions

Immediately following a lesion of either the lateral or ventromedial regions of the hypothalamus, a period of tissue healing and recovery of function ensues. The characteristics of this period differ for lateral and ventromedial lesions. As we have seen, destruction of the lateral hypothalamus renders an animal both aphagic and adipsic: it will neither eat nor drink, and if no nursing is given, it will die within 5 to 10 days. If, on the other hand, the animal is adequately nursed—that is, kept in a comfortably warm environment where he is frequently force-fed through a tube in the stomach—a gradual recovery process begins, resulting in almost complete return to normal eating and drinking within 6 to 70 days.[14,80]

Four distinct recovery phases following lateral hypothalamic lesions have been identified.[79] In *Stage I* animals are adipsic and aphagic: they will not drink or eat any kind of liquid or food. If adequate nursing is not given, they will eventually die. *Stage II* is characterized by adipsia and anorexia. Animals will accept certain types of highly palatable food such as sugar milk, condensed milk, or chocolate milk, but they will still be unable to drink or eat adequate amounts to maintain health. Regular food is completely refused. During *Stage III* the animals are capable of eating and regulating caloric intake when the food presented to them is wet and palatable, but they will refuse to drink water. As long as there is a sufficient amount of liquid in the food, the animals are able to survive. If no liquid is available, the animals become dehydrated and die. *Stage IV,* the recovery stage, is characterized by an apparently normal regulation of food and water intake. The animals are capable of drinking water and eating wet and dry food. However, apparently permanent deficiencies still exist in both water and caloric regulation.[14] Whereas a normal sated animal will eat following an injection of insulin, a lateral-recovered animal will not.[29] In addition, even after reaching *Stage IV* and thereafter, water intake occurs only when associated with eating. The animal reverts to an exaggerated form of its usual prandial (mealtime) drinking, in which a bout of eating is immediately followed by a draft of water.[51]

The stages of feeding recovery after lateral hypothalamic lesions closely resemble the stages of development of feeding observed in the normal newborn animal, and suggest that there is a general parallel between recovery and developmental processes in the nervous system.[81]

Reappearance of eating could be due to any of 3 processes or any combination of them: (a) regeneration of cells—a remote possibility in the nervous system of phylogenetically higher vertebrates; (b) recovery of cells—the lesion does not destroy all of the cells related to a particular function, but leaves some only momentarily knocked out by the traumatic lesioning process; or (c) substitution of cells—other areas of the brain may take over. This last mechanism would be consistent with Lashley's equipotentiality hypothesis [54] and implies that either some other area of the brain can automatically take over the lost function or that, through a developmental and/or learning process, an area of the brain can be trained to perform the function of the recently destroyed tissue. There is some supportive experimental evidence for the last 2 hypotheses.

It has been demonstrated that the extent of the anatomical destruction following a lesion varies greatly, depending on when the autopsy is performed.[89] For instance, if an animal is sacrificed 24 hours after lesioning, a much larger damaged area is discovered than if the animal is sacrificed 10 to 16 days later. Tissue destruction and histological signs of irritation are even less apparent if autopsy is performed several weeks or months after brain lesioning. Whether or not the extent of lesion damage continues to recede over the months that are sometimes involved in the recovery of eating behavior is not known.

The possibility that other brain areas might take over the lost function also has some experimental support.[78] Several rats, upon their recuperation from the aphagia and adipsia produced by lateral lesions of the hypothalamus, were submitted to 24 hours of food deprivation. Then potassium chloride was applied to the surface of the neocortex to depress cortical activity. While in normal animals cortical depression inhibits food and water intake only for a period of from 2 to 24 hours, the lesioned and recuperated animals reverted to early stages of the lateral hypothalamic syndrome for periods of up to 20 days. This suggests that other brain structures, perhaps in the neocortex, may have taken over the function of the damaged hypothalamic area.

The original reports of hyperphagia following ventromedial hypothalamic lesions divided the syndrome into a dynamic and a static phase.[17, 48, 49] The *dynamic phase,* characterized by increased food intake and body weight, may last several weeks or even months. During this phase the consumption of food increases and the animal rapidly gains weight, attaining 2 to 3 times its normal weight. The *static phase* is characterized by an almost normal ingestion of food, and continued obesity. The normal amount of food eaten by the ventromedially lesioned animal in the static phase still reflects a deficiency of regulation. That is, if normal animals are overfed by force-feeding so that comparable obesity results, and food is then made freely available (ad libitum schedule), they will voluntarily stop eating (or reduce it greatly) until their body weight reaches normality. But the hyperphagic animal in the static phase does not cut down food intake in spite of weighing 2 or 3 times as much as a normal animal (see Figure 3–2). Nevertheless, in an unusual way, this animal does regulate his newly acquired body weight. Deprived of food, the hyperphagic-obese animal will lose weight. If it is then placed back on an ad libitum schedule, it will overeat until it reaches the previous level of obesity. Conversely, if force-fed until reaching an even higher body weight and then given ad libitum access to food, it will decrease eating until it attains the previous level of obesity.[45] Thus, a constant body weight is maintained, but at a new and higher-than-normal plateau. There is a recovery of

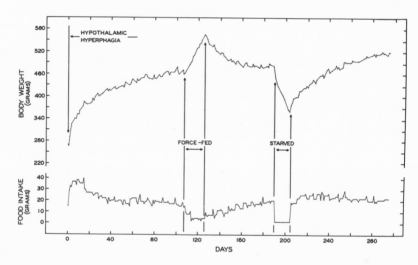

Figure 3–2. Representation of the daily food consumption and body weight of a rat with ventromedial hypothalamic lesions. After reaching the static phase, the animal regulates its body weight even though it is now obese. Forced feeding results in a further increase in body weight. However, if it is discontinued, the rat reduces food intake until its preforced feeding static, obese body weight is reached. Starvation results in a body weight loss, and is followed by overeating when the animal is allowed free feeding. Overeating lasts until its predeprivation static obese body weight is again reached. From B. G. Hoebel and P. Teitelbaum, *J. Comp. Physiol. Psychol.* 61 (1966): 189. Copyright 1966 by the American Psychological Association, and reproduced by permission. Also used by permission of B. G. Hoebel.

function that is abnormal, in that the animal is regulating at a higher body weight. The mechanisms that underlie this phenomenon are not known. Those mechanisms proposed for recovery following lateral hypothalamic lesions may be valid for ventromedial hypothalamic lesions as well.

Some lesions of the ventromedial area result in overeating not because of the primary effect upon the ventromedial satiety center, but because of secondary irritation which stimulates the lateral hypothalamus.[72] If a lesion is made in the ventromedial hypothalamus through a pair of chronically implanted electrodes, the animal develops hyperphagia and goes through the dynamic and static phases of recovery in the usual way. If a second pair of lesions is then made in the same place through the same electrodes, the animal reverts to the dynamic phase, starts overeating, and gains further weight until reaching a second, higher, body weight plateau, at which point it again starts regulating body weight.[43] This finding suggests that the cells surrounding the initial lesions are involved in the partial regulation seen during the initial static phase. It is not clear whether these cells are originally involved in the regulation of food intake, or develop this function secondarily after the original ventromedial lesion.

Changes in Eating Patterns

The patterns of eating of rats following lesions to the ventromedial and lateral hypothalamic areas deviate from those of normal rats. Following lateral hypothalamic lesions, the eating pattern is drastically altered. At first there is no food intake at all. But when the animal regains eating ability, the several changes that develop in the way it eats its meals are related to food intake and to water intake.[50] The recovered animal increases the number of meals, but decreases the size of each meal. Thus, although the animal eats sufficient dry food to maintain a constant body weight, it exhibits an abnormal feeding pattern, becoming a nibbler. Furthermore, this nibbling is accompanied by excessive spillage; almost half of what is chewed is spilled out. The water intake pattern of this animal is also altered. It becomes a pronounced prandial drinker, continuously interrupting eating to have small drafts of water. Since an animal from which the salivary glands have been removed shows normal eating patterns, except for increased prandial drinking, the change in meal size and frequency in the recovered lateral lesioned animal is not caused by the decrease in saliva production that normally results from lesioning the lateral hypothalamus.

More details are known about the results of lesioning the ventromedial hypothalamus. Lesions in this nucleus produce hyperphagia in both male and female rats,[12] although weight gain is more exaggerated in females.[85] During the immediate postoperative period, rats display an increase in general activity that lasts for a few hours and is then replaced by chronic hypoactivity. Even then, however, they remain hyperreactive to external stimulation.[12, 19, 22] On the basis of the feeding patterns of ventromedially lesioned subjects, it is possible to distinguish three periods: an *acute* dynamic period, a *chronic* dynamic period, and finally the static period.[12]

From the time a ventromedial lesioned animal begins recovering from surgical anesthesia, and for about 12 hours thereafter, a single, extended bout of eating is commonly observed. This persistent eating gradually condenses into discrete meals, as depicted in Figure 3–3. As can be seen, the initial changes are more exaggerated in the male than in the female. The prolonged feeding cannot be attributed to any general impairment produced by surgical manipulation, since sham-operated animals show only a transient and light disturbance in eating patterns. The behavior of the lesioned animals is an exaggeration of the behavior observed in control rats that have been deprived of food for 36 to 52 hours. When such animals are given access to food, they also exhibit a prolonged bout of eating. But the similarity between the ventromedially lesioned rats and the deprived ones is only superficial. The ventromedially lesioned rats are much

Hypothalamic Control

POST-OPERATIVE FEEDING PATTERNS

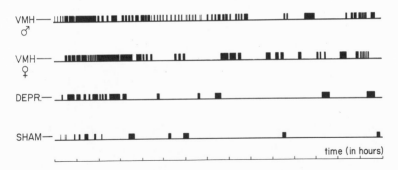

Figure 3–3. Actual feeding records of the eating activity of animals submitted to lesions of the ventromedial hypothalamus (VMH; ♂ = male; ♀ = female), 52 hours of food deprivation (DEPR.), or surgical stress without lesioning the ventromedial nucleus (SHAM). The records should be read from left to right. Each pen deflection represents 1 feeding response. From S. Balagura and L. D. Devenport, *J. Comp. Physiol. Psychol.* 71 (1970): 357. Used by permission.

more ravenous; unlike lesioned animals, deprived rats typically resume normal eating 1 to 3 hours after surgery. Ventromedial hypothalamic lesions thus produce a more sustained initial period of eating (the acute dynamic phase) than do 36 to 52 hours of food deprivation.

What has been typically described as the dynamic phase of hyperphagia [19] corresponds to the chronic dynamic period. The activity of the animals is greatly reduced, they are hyperreactive to external stimulation, and eating is characterized by discrete meals. Several changes occur in the number, size, and distribution of meals during a given 24-hour period,[12] as illustrated in Figure 3–4. The number of meals increases for both sexes. When exposed to cycles of 12 hours of light and 12 hours of dark, male rats eat more meals during *both* periods of the light-dark cycle, while female rats eat a great many more meals during the light period and a normal number during the dark period. Female rats eat much larger meals during both light and dark periods, but the meal size for males is the same as for normal rats. The interval between meals is greatly affected in both sexes by ventromedial lesions. The

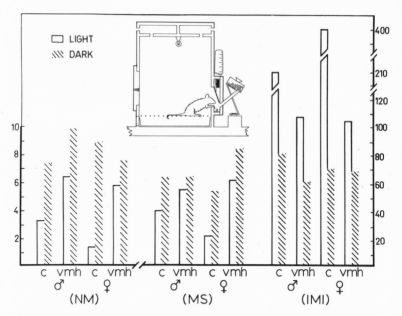

Figure 3–4. Histogram of mean number of meals (NM), average meal size (MS), and intermeal intervals in minutes (IMI) of male and female rats with and without lesions of the ventromedial hypothalamus. C = control animals, vmh = animals with lesions of the ventromedial hypothalamus. From S. Balagura and L. D. Devenport, *J. Comp. Physiol. Psychol.* 71 (1970): 357. Used by permission.

duration of the intermeal interval during the daytime decreases by about 60 percent, and there is a tendency for it to decrease somewhat during the night as well. The ventromedial hypothalamus is thus involved not only in the regulation of meal size, but also helps regulate the circadian rhythm of feeding activity.

Feeding Finickiness

Several changes in taste preferences occur after hypothalamic lesions. The subject becomes hyper-reactive to flavors to the point of interference with caloric regulation. The influence of taste during the recovery stages following lateral hypothalamic damage has already been considered. A fully recovered lateral lesioned animal would die of starvation rather than eat a nonpalatable food.[79, 87] If bitter quinine is added to its water—in amounts tolerated by normal subjects—a rat which has recuperated from lateral lesions refuses to drink and dies of severe dehydration.

Following ventromedial lesioning, the animal's motivation to obtain food is also changed. Initially the animal is extremely active in obtaining food, but while food intake remains excessive during the prolonged period of weight gain, the animal's motivation to work for food soon wanes to a level lower than that for normal animals. If a lesioned animal, for example, is maintained at a body weight below its preoperative level, the animal will press a bar to obtain food at a higher than normal rate. As obesity develops, however, motivation for food decreases. The animal bar presses less for food, decreases running speed in an alley that leads to food, and is less willing to tolerate electrical shock in order to obtain food.[24, 60, 76]

During the dynamic phase of hyperphagia, food intake is maintained despite adulteration of the diet with unpalatable materials. During the static phase, however, the animal becomes finicky and rejects such adulterated diets to a degree that becomes disadvantageous to the regulation of energy balance, and may even lead to death. Even changes in the texture of the food become important determinants of eating behavior (e.g., powdered versus hard food). Just as the animal is hypersensitive to the negative aspects of its diet, it is also hypersensitive to the positive aspects, and will overeat when given a highly palatable liquid or solid. This finickiness has suggested that the increased feeding may be solely due to an intensification of the taste aspects of food.[77] According to this idea, the animal becomes hyperphagic not because of a primary disturbance in eating behavior but because of secondary changes in taste preference.[32, 34] However, such a mechanism cannot account for the entire hyperphagic syndrome. When animals are trained to self-inject food directly into their stomachs, by-passing their mouths and completely eliminating taste, they still overeat and become obese.[59]

Hypothalamic Self-Stimulation

In 1954 Olds described for the first time his classic finding of hypothalamic self-stimulation: [63] When electrodes are implanted in the hypothalamus of animals and the experimental situation is such that pressing a bar delivers a train of small electrical pulses to their brains, the animals learn to bar press within a very short time. They become hard workers, bar pressing at rates up to 6,000 times per hour, for hours and hours. Such a rate cannot be achieved with any other rewards such as food or water. Hundreds of subsequent self-stimulation experiments have made it clear that a motivational–reward system can be activated by electrical stimulation of the hypothalamus. It has been hypothesized that this system is functionally related to the hypothalamic systems that mediate eating and drinking.[11, 61]

It was not until 1962 that this motivation–reward system was experimentally related to eating behavior. If an animal is made hungry by being deprived of food for several hours and then allowed to electrically self-stimulate its lateral hypothalamus, its rate of bar pressing is higher than the rate prior to deprivation.[57] On the other hand, if the animal is force-fed until sated, the self-stimulation rate decreases.[44] The relationship between self-stimulation rate and eating behavior is not limited to the actual state of deprivation or satiation of the animal, in terms of time since eating, but is also related to hormonal systems normally involved in the regulation of eating behavior and energy metabolism.[13] Insulin, a pancreatic hormone which induces animals to eat, also increases the self-stimulation rate. Glucagon, another pancreatic hormone which decreases eating in animals, decreases the rate of self-stimulation. Furthermore, intragastric injections of concentrated glucose, which normally terminate eating, also decrease self-stimulation.[10] It appears that the self-stimulation reward system of the lateral hypothalamus is related to a system which helps regulate eating behavior, and depends in part on the levels of the organism's glucose energy.

Other Hypothalamic Functions

The hypothalamus has many functions in addition to those related to eating and drinking behavior. It is involved in regulation of blood pressure and heart rate,[46, 86] as well as exerting influence on the blood vessels of the respiratory system.[30] The movement,[16, 47, 58] as well as the secretions,[55, 68] of the gastrointestinal system are also in part controlled by the hypothalamus.

The hypothalamus is also involved in the regulation of body temperature. The anterior hypothalamus helps shape the body's adaptive responses to an increase in environmental temperature,[15, 56] while the posterior hypothalamus is involved in physiological responses to a cold environment.[71]

Another function of the hypothalamus concerns the regulation and production of several hormones of the hypothalamic–hypophyseal system.[27, 39] Certain lesions of the hypothalamus are followed by the atrophy and degeneration of the gonads and external genitalia, and the disruption of body growth and fat metabolism. The hypothalamus contains a series of hormonal-releasing factors indispensable for the normal function of the hypophysis.

Just as the hypothalamus is involved in the regulation of many different functions, other brain structures have been shown to share with the hypothalamus the regulation of eating behavior. The following chapter considers these in detail.

BIBLIOGRAPHY

1. Albert, D. J., and Storlien, L. H. Hyperphagia in rats with cuts between the ventromedial and lateral hypothalamus. *Science* 165 (1969): 599–600.

2. Anand, B. K., and Brobeck, J. R. Hypothalamic control of food intake in rats and cats. *Yale J. Biol. Med.* 24 (1951): 123–140.

3. ———. Localization of a feeding center in the hypothalamus of the rat. *Proc. Soc. Exp. Biol. Med.* 77 (1951): 323–324.

4. Anand, B. K., and Dua, S. Feeding responses induced by electrical stimulation of hypothalamus in cat. *Indian J. Med. Res.* 43 (1955): 113–122.

5. Anand, B. K.; Chhina, G. S.; and Singh, B. Effect of glucose on the activity of hypothalamic "feeding centers." *Science* 138 (1962): 597–598.

6. Anand, B. K.; Chhina, G. S.; Sharma, K.; Dua, S.; and Singh, B. Activity of single neurons in hypothalamic feeding centers: effect of glucose. *Amer. J. Physiol.* 207 (1964): 1145–1154.

7. Anliker, J., and Mayer, J. An operant conditioning technique for studying feeding-fasting patterns in normal and obese mice. *J. Appl. Physiol.* 8 (1956): 667–670.

8. Arees, E. A., and Mayer, J. Anatomical connections between medial and lateral regions of the hypothalamus concerned with food intake. *Science* 157 (1967): 1574–1575.

9. Bailey, P., and Bremer, F. Experimental diabetes insipidus. *Arch. intern. Med.* 28 (1921): 773–803.

10. Balagura, S. Influence of osmotic and caloric loads upon lateral hypothalamic self-stimulation. *J. Comp. Physiol. Psychol.* 66 (1968), 325–328.

11. ———. Neurochemical regulation of food intake. In *The hypothalamus,* ed. L. Martini, M. Motta, and F. Fraschini, pp. 181–193. London: Academic Press, 1970.

12. ———, and Devenport, L. D. Feeding patterns of normal and ventromedial hypothalamic lesioned male and female rats. *J. Comp. Physiol. Psychol.* 71 (1970): 357–364.

13. Balagura, S., and Hoebel, B. G. Self-stimulation of the lateral hypothalamus modified by insulin and glucagon. *Physiol. Behav.* 2 (1967): 337–340.

14. Balagura, S.; Wilcox, R. H.; and Coscina, D. V. The effect of diencephalic lesions on food intake and motor activity. *Physiol. Behavior* 4 (1969): 629–633.

15. Beaton, L. E.; Leininger, C.; McKinley, W. A.; Magoun, H. W.; and Ranson, S. W. Neurogenic hyperthermia and its treatment with soluble pentobarbital in the monkey. *Arch. Neurol. Psychiat.* 49 (1943): 518–536.

16. Beattie, J., and Sheehan, D. The effects of hypothalamic stimulation on gastric motility. *J. Physiol. (London)* 81 (1934): 218–277.

17. Brobeck, J. R. Mechanism of the development of obesity in animals with hypothalamic lesions. *Physiol. Rev.* 26 (1946): 541–559.

18. ———, Tepperman, J.; and Long, C. N. H. Effect of experimental obesity upon carbohydrate metabolism. *Yale J. Biol. Med.* 15 (1943): 893–904.

19. ———. Experimental hypothalamic hyperphagia in the rat. *Yale J. Biol. Med.* 15 (1943): 830–853.

20. Brooks, C. Mc. A study of the respiratory quotient in experimental hypothalamic obesity. *Amer. J. Physiol.* 147 (1946): 727–734.

21. ———, and Lambert, E. F. A study of the effect of limitation of food intake and the method of feeding on the rate of weight gain during hypothalamic obesity in the albino rat. *Amer. J. Physiol.* 147 (1946): 695–707.

22. Brooks, C. Mc.; Lockwood, R. A.; and Wiggins, M. L. A study of the effect of hypothalamic lesions on the eating habits of the albino rat. *Amer. J. Physiol.* 147 (1946): 735–742.

23. Brügger, M. Fresstrieb als hypothalamisches Symptom. *Helv. Physiol. Pharmacol. Acta* 1 (1943): 183–198.

24. Coons, E. E., and Quartermain, D. Motivational depression associated with norepinephrine-induced eating from the hypothalamus: resem-

blance to the ventromedial hyperphagic syndrome. *Physiol. Behav.* 5 (1970): 687–692.

25. Coons, E. E.; Levak, M.; and Miller, N. E. Lateral hypothalamus: Learning of food-seeking response motivated by electrical stimulation. *Science* 150 (1965): 1320–1321.

26. Delgado, J. M. R., and Anand, B. K. Increase in food intake induced by electrical stimulation of the lateral hypothalamus. *Amer. J. Physiol.* 172 (1953): 162–168.

27. Donovan, B. T. Experimental lesions of the hypothalamus: a critical survey with particular reference to endocrine effects. *Brit. Med. Bull.* 22 (1966): 249–253.

28. Epstein, A. N. Reciprocal changes in feeding behavior produced by intrahypothalamic chemical injections. *Amer. J. Physiol.* 199 (1960): 969–974.

29. ――――, and Teitelbaum, P. Specific loss of the hypoglycemic control of feeding in recovered lateral rats. *Amer. J. Physiol.* 213 (1967): 1159–1167.

30. Gamble, J. E., and Patton, H. D. Pulmonary edema and hemorrhage from preoptic lesions in rats. *Amer. J. Physiol.* 172 (1953): 623–631.

31. Gold, R. M. Aphagia and adipsia produced by unilateral hypothalamic lesions in rats. *Amer. J. Physiol.* 211 (1966): 1274–1276.

32. Graff, H., and Stellar, E. Hyperphagia, obesity, and finickiness. *J. Comp. Physiol. Psychol.* 55 (1962): 918–924.

33. Grimm, R. J. Feeding behavior and electrical stimulation of the brain of *Carassius auratus*. *Science* 131 (1960): 162.

34. Grossman, S. P. The VMH: A center for affective reactions, satiety, or both? *Physiol. Behav.* 1 (1966): 1–10.

35. Hamilton, C., and Brobeck, J. Hypothalamic hyperphagia in the monkey. *J. Comp. Physiol. Psychol.* 57 (1964): 271–278.

36. Han, P. W. Hypothalamic obesity in rats without hyperphagia. *Trans. N. Y. Acad. Sci.* 30 (1967): 229–243.

37. ――――, and Liu, A. C. Body fat content and linear growth of rats force-fed for forty days after hypothalamic lesions. *Fed. Proc.* 25 (1966): 192 (Abst. 19).

38. Hardwood, D., and Vowles, D. M. Forebrain stimulation and feeding behavior in the ring dove (*streptopelia risoria*). *J. Comp. Physiol. Psychol.* 62 (1966): 388–396.

39. Heller, H. The hormone content of the vertebrate hypothalamo-neurohypophyseal system. *Brit. Med. Bull.* 22 (1966): 227–231.

40. Hetherington, A. W., and Ranson, S. W. Experimental hypothalamo-hypophyseal obesity in the rat. *Proc. Soc. Biol. Med.* 41 (1939): 465–466.

41. ――――, and Ranson, S. W. Hypothalamic lesions and adiposity in the rat. *Anat. Rec.* 78 (1940): 149–172.

42. ――――. Hypothalamus lesions and adiposity. *J. com. Neurol.* 76 (1942): 475–499.

43. Hoebel, B. G. Feeding and self-stimulation. *Ann. N. Y. Acad. Sci.* 157 (1969): 758–778.

44. ――――, and Teitelbaum, P. Hypothalamic control of feeding and self-stimulation. *Science* 135 (1962): 375–377.

45. ――――. Weight regulation in normal and hypothalamic hyperphagic rats. *J. Comp. Physiol. Psychol.* 61 (1966): 189–193.

46. Kabat, H.; Magoun, H. W.; and Ranson, S. W. Electrical stimulation of points in the forebrain and midbrain. The resultant alterations in blood pressure. *Arch. Neurol. Psychiat.* 34 (1935): 931–955.

47. ———; and Anson, B. J. Stimulation of the hypothalamus with special reference to its effect on gastro-intestinal motility. *Amer. J. Physiol.* 112 (1935): 214–226.

48. Kennedy, G. C. Food intake, energy balance and growth. *Brit. Med. Bull.* 22 (1966): 216–220.

49. ———. The hypothalamic control of food intake in rats. *Proc. Roy. Soc. (London), B* 137 (1950): 535–548.

50. Kissileff, H. R. Free feeding in normal and "recovered lateral" rats monitored by a pellet-detecting eatometer. *Physiol. Behav.* 5 (1970): 163–173.

51. ———, and Epstein, A. N. Exaggerated prandial drinking in the "recovered lateral" rat without saliva. *J. Comp. Physiol. Psychol.* 67 (1969): 301–308.

52. Krasne, F. B. General disruption resulting from electrical stimulus of ventromedial hypothalamus. *Science* 138 (1962): 822–823.

53. Larsson, S. On the hypothalamic organization of the nervous mechanism regulating food intake. *Acta Physiol. Scand.* 32 (1954): Suppl. 115, 1–63.

54. Lashley, K. S. *Brain mechanisms and intelligence.* New York: Dover Publications, 1963.

55. Lepkovsky, S., and Dimick, M. K. The hypothalamus and pancreas in intestinal function. *Ann. N. Y. Acad. Sci.* 157 (1969): 1062–1068.

56. Magoun, H. W.; Harrison, F.; Brobeck, J. R.; and Ranson, S. W. Activation of heat loss mechanisms by local heatings of the brain. *J. Neurophysiol.* 1 (1938): 101–114.

57. Margules, D. L., and Olds, J. Identical "feeding" and "reward" systems in the lateral hypothalamus of rats. *Science* 135 (1962): 374.

58. Masserman, J. H., and Haertig, E. W. The influence of hypothalamic stimulation on intestinal activity. *J. Neurophysiol.* 1 (1938): 350–356.

59. McGinty, D.; Epstein, A. N.; and Teitelbaum, P. The contribution of oropharyngeal sensations to hypothalamic hyperphagia. *Animal Behaviour* 13 (1965): 413–418.

60. Miller, N. E.; Bailey, C. J.; and Stevenson, J. A. F. Decreased hunger but increased food intake resulting from hypothalamic lesions. *Science* 112 (1950): 256–259.

61. Mogenson, G. J., and Stevenson, J. A. F. Drinking and self-stimulation with electrical stimulation of the lateral hypothalamus. *Physiol. Behav.* 1 (1966): 251–254.

62. ———. Drinking induced by electrical stimulation of the lateral hypothalamus. *Exp. Neurol.* 17 (1967): 119–127.

63. Olds, J., and Milner, P. Positive reinforcement produced by electrical stimulation of the septal area and other regions of rat brain. *J. Comp. Physiol. Psychol.* 47 (1954): 419–427.

64. Oomura, Y. H.; Ooyama, T.; Yamamoto, T.; and Naka, F. Reciprocal relationship of the lateral and ventromedial hypothalamus in the regulation of food intake. *Physiol. Behav.* 2 (1967): 97–115.

65. Oomura, Y.; Ooyama, H.; Yamamoto, T.; Ono, T.; and Kobayashi, N. Behavior of hypothalamic unit activity during electrophoretic application of drugs. *Ann. N. Y. Acad. Sci.* 157 (1969): 642–689.

66. Oomura, Y.; Kimura, K.; Ooyama, H.; Maeno, T.; Iki, M.; and Kuniyoshi, M. Reciprocal activities of the ventromedial and lateral hypothalamic areas of cats. *Science* 143 (1964): 484–485.

67. Pool, R. Suction lesions and hypothalamic hyperphagia. *Amer. J. Physiol.* 213 (1967): 31–35.

68. Porter, R. W.; Movius, H. J.; and French, J. D. Hypothalamic influences on hydrochloric acid secretion of the stomach. *Surgery* 33 (1953): 875–880.

69. Powley, T. L., and Keesey, R. E. Relationship of body weight to the lateral hypothalamic feeding syndrome. *J. Comp. Physiol. Psychol.* 70 (1970): 25–36.

70. Rabin, M. M., and Smith, C. J. Behavioral comparison of the effectiveness of irritative and non-irritative lesions in producing hypothalamic hyperphagia. *Physiol. Behav.* 3 (1968): 417–420.

71. Ranson, S. W. Regulation of body temperature. *Res. Publ. Ass. nerv. ment. Dis.* 20 (1940): 342–399.

72. Reynolds, R. W. Radio frequency lesions in the ventrolateral hypothalamic "feeding center." *J. Comp. Physiol. Psychol.* 56 (1963): 965–967.

73. Robinson, B. W., and Mishkin, M. Alimentary responses evoked from forebrain structures in *Macaca mulata*. *Science* 136 (1962): 260–262.

74. Smith, O. A. Food intake and HT stimulation. In *Electrical stimulation of the brain,* ed. D. E. Sheer. Austin: Univ. of Texas Press, 1961.

75. Stellar, E. The physiology of motivation. *Psychol. Rev.* 61 (1954): 5–22.

76. Teitelbaum, P. Random and food-directed activity in hyperphagic and normal rats. *J. Comp. Physiol. Psychol.* 50 (1957): 486–490.

77. ———. Sensory control of hypothalamic hyperphagia. *J. Comp. Physiol. Psychol.* 48 (1955): 156–163.

78. ———, and Cytawa, J. Spreading depression and recovery from lateral hypothalamic lesions. *Science* 147 (1965): 61–63.

79. Teitelbaum, P., and Epstein, A. N. The lateral hypothalamic syndrome. *Psychol. Rev.* 69 (1962): 74–90.

80. Teitelbaum, P., and Stellar, E. Recovery from the failure to eat produced by hypothalamic lesions. *Science* 120 (1954): 894–895.

81. Teitelbaum, P., Cheng, M. F., and Rozin, P. Development of feeding parallels its recovery after hypothalamic damage. *J. Comp. Physiol. Psychol.* 67 (1969): 430–441.

82. Tepperman, J.; Brobeck, J. R.; and Long, C. N. H. The effects of hypothalamic hyperphagia and of alterations in feeding habits on the metabolism of the albino rat. *Yale J. Biol. Med.* 15 (1943): 855–879.

83. Ungestedt, U. Adipsia and aphagia after 6-hydroxydopamine induced degeneration of the nigro-striatal dopamine system. *Acta Physiol. Scand.* suppl. 567 (1971): 95–122.

84. Valenstein, E. S.; Cox, V. C.; and Kakolewski, J. W. Hypothalamic motivational systems: fixed or plastic neural circuits? *Science* 163 (1969): 1084.

85. ———. Sex differences in hyperphagia and body weight following hypothalamic damage. *Ann. N. Y. Acad. Sci.* 157 (1969): 1030–1046.

86. Wang, S. C., and Ranson, S. W. The role of the hypothalamus and preoptic region in the regulation of heart rate. *Amer. J. Physiol.* 132 (1941): 5–8.

87. Williams, D. R., and Teitelbaum, P. Some observations on the star-

vation resulting from lateral hypothalamic lesions. *J. Comp. Physiol. Psychol.* 52 (1959): 458–465.

88. Wise, R. A. Hypothalamic motivational systems: fixed or plastic neural circuits? *Science* 162 (1968): 377–379.

89. Wolf, G., and DiCara, L. Progressive morphologic changes in electrolytic brain lesions. *Exp. Neurol.* 23 (1969): 529–536.

90. Wyrwicka, W., and Dobrzecka, C. Relationship between feeding and satiation centers of the hypothalamus. *Science* 131 (1960): 805–806.

SUGGESTED SUPPLEMENTARY READINGS

Anand, B. K. Nervous regulation of food intake. *Physiol. Rev.* 41 (1961): 677–708.

Balagura, S. Hypothalamic factors in the control of eating behavior. *Adv. Psychosom. Med.* 7 (1972): 25–48.

Valenstein, E. S. The anatomical locus of reinforcement. In *Progress in physiological psychology,* ed. E. Stellar and J. M. Sprague, pp. 149–185. New York: Academic Press, 1967.

———; Cox, V. C.; and Kakolewski, J. W. Reexamination of the role of the hypothalamus in motivation. *Psychol. Rev.* 77 (1970): 16–31.

CHAPTER 4

Extrahypothalamic Regulation

Some brain structures outside the hypothalamus are thought capable of influencing food intake. The amygdala, the hippocampus, the septal area, the limbic cortex, the temporal lobe, and the extrapyramidal and brainstem areas have received the major experimental attention. Presently, there is no clear understanding of the precise role extrahypothalamic structures may play in the regulation of food intake. Exploration of extrahypothalamic mechanisms, however, has become important in the study of the neural basis of feeding behavior.

Interest in extrahypothalamic structures arose mainly for 2 reasons. First, a number of experiments not concerned with feeding behavior unexpectedly revealed changes in food intake following damage to a variety of CNS structures. Second, researchers became frustrated with their inability to account for the full neural control of eating through hypothalamic mechanisms alone. Originally, investigators had believed that study of the hypothalamus would answer the majority of questions raised about feeding behavior. However, as this research grew in complexity, it became evident that the hypothalamus could not be the sole regulator of feeding. Scientists accordingly began to consider additional neural structures for basic explanations of feeding behavior, with special attention being paid to structures within or along the limbic system.

For many years most of the limbic structures, the cingulate, subcallosal and frontotemporal cortex, septal area, prepyriform and amygdaloid complex, hippocampus, and olfactory complex, were thought to be involved primarily in olfactory functions. This assumption seemed plausible, since all of the structures in question possessed either direct or indirect connections to the olfactory bulbs. In fact, many of the limbic structures were collectively designated as the *rhinencephalon* (smell- or nose-brain). However, experiments correlating behavioral changes with neural damage indicated that destruction of many of these structures, and a number of the connecting pathways among them, had minimal or nonexistent effects on the sense of smell. In short, it appeared that olfaction per se is not a critical function subserved by the limbic system.

In the late 1930s, when the role of the limbic system in olfaction was being questioned, the anatomist Papez concluded that a number of limbic structures—notably the hippocampus, entorhinal and cingulate cortex, the septal region, and the amygdala, in conjunction with parts of the thalamus and hypothalamus—mediated emotional behavior.[40] Almost simultaneously, Klüver and Bucy [27,28] described a behavioral syndrome in monkeys which had sustained bilateral lesions in the temporal lobes involving some underlying limbic structures. Their findings provided behavioral support for the notions of Papez. Their monkeys showed a decrease in fear and anger, becoming much tamer and approaching objects and people with great curiosity. They also had an increased propensity to examine things orally, as well as an increase in food consumption. More recently, this same syndrome has been reported in humans.[55] Shortly after the therapeutic extirpation of the temporal lobes, some patients display pronounced memory deficits, an increase in the manipulation of objects, decreased emotionality, and an insatiable appetite.

While these gross behavioral changes following massive temporal lobe damage did not permit workers to specify the function of discrete neural areas, they did reveal a striking variety of behavioral functions within the limbic system. Although more recent research has localized the structures involved in a number of these behavioral changes reported over 3 decades ago, it was the pioneering work of Papez and Klüver and Bucy that gave birth to the interest in extrahypothalamic mechanisms of food intake.

Temporal Lobe and Amygdala

Experiments performed in the latter part of the nineteenth century, while having little impact on subsequent research, had shown that hyperphagia occurred in monkeys following temporal lobe destruction. As we have seen, the work of Klüver and Bucy in the late 1930s brought these findings to life once again. These workers noted that, aside from the increase of their monkeys' oral manipulation and food intake, the lesioned animals also developed preference changes in their regular diet. Some of the monkeys, normally herbivorous, became carnivorous, consuming foodstuffs such as bacon, ham, and sausage. Baboons and rhesus monkeys react the same way (as the monkeys cited above) to temporal lobe damage and, when the amygdala is also lesioned, become obese as well.[43] Such effects on eating behavior are not limited to primates. In the cat, for example, surgical damage to the amygdala produces an increase in food intake to the extent that an animal increases body weight as much as 30 percent within a 40-day period.[16] Similar changes in food intake can also be produced in the rat.[19]

Since these earlier experiments produced widespread damage to both the temporal lobes and amygdala, a great variety of behavioral changes occurred. It is now known, however, that lesions limited to the central and medial parts of the amygdala can produce a 4-fold increase of food intake in cats.[58] Lesions of the pyriform cortex, which immediately underlies the amygdala, along with amygdalar damage, can also result in persistent hyperphagia and an increased rate of weight gain.[35, 36]

As might be expected, the amygdala and ventromedial hypothalamus appear to work together in keeping food intake down to a normal level. Combined lesions of the 2 structures produce a greater hyperphagia than that observed after either lesion alone.[37] It is possible that both the amygdala and the ventromedial hypothalamus have an inhibitory influence upon some third structure, such as the lateral hypothalamus. Lesions of both of these structures thus would lead to a greater reduction of inhibition than from either lesion alone, with a consequent greater increase in food intake.

While aphagia, anorexia, and body weight loss may occur after amygdalar destruction, [16,29] some workers have reported no observable changes in food intake after such lesions.[1,25] This discrepancy is apparently dependent on the species of animal studied. Amygdalar damage has no effect in monkeys, produces mild anorexia in cats, and results in prolonged anorexia in rats.[26] As one ascends the phylogenetic scale, the amygdala seemingly becomes less important with respect to regulation of food intake. Nevertheless, in humans,[39,49,55] as well as in monkeys,[51] hyperphagia has been reported following ablation of the amygdala. It may be that different areas of the amygdala were lesioned in the various experiments. When evaluating the involvement of the amygdala in feeding regulation, it is necessary to consider specific nuclei within it which may have different functions in feeding.

Most electrical stimulation studies support the contention that the amygdala is involved in regulation of food intake. As early as 1953, MacLean and Delgado showed that electrical stimulation of the amygdala in cats and monkeys produces responses such as sniffing, licking, biting, chewing, and gagging.[31] Such fragmentary responses are known as "eating automatisms." Fullblown hyperphagia, however, has also been induced in both monkeys and rats by electrical stimulation of the amygdala.[19,46] It appears that a diffuse feeding system may be located throughout the amygdaloid complex. As with lesions, however, electrical stimulation of the amygdala has not always resulted in an increase of food intake, and sometimes an actual decrease in eating has been observed.[12,14]

The neural pathways involved in amygdalar control of eating

behavior are not known for certain. When the effects of electrical stimulation of the amygdala among rats with and without ventromedial hypothalamic lesions were compared, it appeared that the amygdala might operate through the ventromedial hypothalamus.[57] That is, stimulation of the amygdala in the presence of the ventromedial hypothalamus led to inhibition of eating, but stimulation after ventromedial hypothalamic ablation did not. This would be an alternative arrangement to the possibility that the ventromedial hypothalamus and the amygdala operate upon a third system to inhibit feeding.[37]

It does not seem that the amygdala functions as a homogeneous system, since both lesioning and stimulation can increase eating behavior. It appears more likely that 2 or more systems are scattered diffusely throughout the amygdaloid complex. Thus, lesioning of 1 system could result in an increase of eating, while stimulation of another could have a similar effect. Such a diffuse structural and/or functional representation within the amygdaloid complex could account for some of the contradictions about its role in feeding behavior.

The functions of the amygdaloid complex have also been studied through the use of chemical rather than electrical stimulation.[17] Deposition of both adrenergic and cholinergic compounds in the amygdala fail to elicit feeding or drinking in sated animals. However, a markedly facilitating effect on feeding occurs when adrenergic substances are injected after the animals have been deprived of food for 24 hours. Norepinephrine increases food intake while cholinergic substances increase drinking. It seems that some components of the amygdala exert effects on feeding only when other parts of the brain concerned with food intake are activated, as is the case in the deprived state.

Hippocampus

Most studies of the hippocampus have yielded inconsistent results. In the rat, for example, electrolytic lesions of the hippocampus are sometimes followed by no changes in feeding habits,[3, 38] and sometimes by an increase in food consumption.[9, 42] Some investigators blame species or strain differences, but inconsistent findings have even been reported within the same strain of rats. These conflicting results may be due to differences in localization of the lesions; the hippocampus is a large, elongated structure, and many times different hippocampal components have been lesioned. It is also possible that other brain structures are damaged during the hippocampal surgery. Recently, for example, it has been shown that destruction of the entorhinal cortex, neighboring the hippocampus, enhances food intake.[10]

The enhanced food intake sometimes reported after hippocampal lesions may not be due to a direct effect on a feeding system, since the hippocampus is known to be associated with response inhibition.[8] Animals with hippocampal lesions thus have trouble suppressing a variety of response patterns even when responding is no longer reinforced. They are deficient in passive avoidance tasks, overactive in their operant responding for food, and even hyperactive in open-field activity tests. Therefore, it is possible that the overeating following hippocampal damage may reflect general response perseverance rather than a specific increase in hunger.

Electrical stimulation of the hippocampus can produce eating behavior.[34] If rats are trained to stimulate their own dorso-lateral hippocampus electrically, and food is available during or after stimulation, they increase their food intake. Moreover, if they have to obtain their food by pressing a bar, they press more often *following* hippocampal stimulation. This suggests that the eating produced by hippocampal stimulation results from an after-discharge either in the hippocampus or some other structure, activated by hippocampal stimulation.

An increase in food intake has also been observed after chemical stimulation of the hippocampus.[6, 15] Norepinephrine, known to elicit eating when injected into other limbic and diencephalic structures, has the same effect when injected into the dorsal or ventral hippocampus. The effect is usually weak, and may result from the chemical spreading to neighboring areas.

Septal Area

This brain structure, part of the limbic system, has extensive connections with the hypothalamus and other limbic structures and may participate in the regulation of feeding behavior. Behavioral interest in the septum, as it is sometimes called, only arose in the early 1960s, and while few investigators have yet studied the effects of septal manipulation on food intake, some facts are known. Septal lesions in rats, which result in a strong hyperdipsia, also moderately enhance food consumption and operant responding for food.[7, 52] The lateral septum may be more important than the medial septum in the regulation of feeding. When the medial area is lesioned, the primary and most noticeable changes occur in emotional reactivity and drinking behavior, and some of the changes observed in feeding behavior may result from an attempt to adapt to the changes in drinking behavior.[7] Furthermore, the septum is intimately connected with the hippocampus, and also plays a role in general response inhibition.[22, 33] The increase in operant responding for food, as well as overeating, could thus reflect the animal's inability to inhibit food oriented responses.

When hyperphagia follows lesions of the septum, the animals are also finicky. When presented with dry or cellulose adulterated food, they decrease their intake. Only lesions of the posterior septum produce a finicky response to water adulterated with quinine, while both anterior and posterior lesions render an animal positively overreactive to a highly palatable saccharin solution.[4] Whether the changes observed after septal damage—changes which resemble a mild ventromedial hypothalamic syndrome—

reflect secondary alterations in ventromedial hypothalamic function or an alteration of some regulatory process shared by both structures is yet to be determined.[24]

Chemical stimulation of the septum changes water intake and perhaps food intake. Cholinergic stimulation is followed by drinking and a depression of eating in hungry animals.[18] Norepinephrine injections are followed by an increase in feeding,[6] especially when the lateral septal area is stimulated.

The septal area constitutes one of the origins of the stria medullaris. Some of the fibers of the latter are connected to the thalamus. Electrical stimulation of the thalamus has been found to increase food intake,[32, 53] whereas lesioning of it may result in aphagia, although in some cases more discrete lesions can induce hyperphagia.[48, 50] Injections of norepinephrine have been shown to induce feeding.[6] These findings support the contention that structures connected by the stria medullaris, such as the lateral septum and the thalamus, represent part of a feeding system parallel and complementary to the lateral-ventromedial hypothalamic feeding system.[5]

Limbic Cortices

Separate from the neocortex, which covers most of the cerebrum, there is a more primitive form of cortex which covers portions of the base of the hemispheres as well as their medial surface. Known as limbic cortices, they include the pyriform and entorhinal cortices beneath the hemispheres and the cingulate cortex above the corpus callosum on the medial surface of the brain. Considered along with these structures will be the frontal lobes, which, though strictly neocortical, have important connections with the limbic system.

Electrical stimulation of the pyriform cortex elicits sniffing, biting, chewing, licking, swallowing, and salivation in a broad range of vertebrates, from the fish to the monkey.[22, 23, 45] However, discrete electrolytic lesions confined solely to the pyriform cortex fail to modify food intake. It is possible that the pyriform region is not involved in the basic regulation of food intake, but indirectly influences the eating process as a result of its close association with the olfactory system. By contrast, damage to the entorhinal cortex, immediately behind the pyriform area, produces a moderate but transitory hyperphagia lasting 3 weeks.[10] The degree of hyperphagia and obesity is closely related to the size of the entorhinal lesion.

The influence of the cingulate cortex is apparently in the same direction as that of the lateral hypothalamus. Although some investigators have reported no alterations in feeding as a result of either cingulate lesions or stimulation,[2, 12, 34] others have reported increased eating during electrical stimulation,[46] and decreased feeding following its ablation.[30] As in the lateral hypothalamus, chemical stimulation of the cingulate region with norepinephrine elicits eating, while stimulation with carbachol, a cholinergic agent, elicits drinking.[6, 11]

Frontal lobotomy, the sectioning of the major connections to the frontal lobes, increases food consumption in humans.[20, 21] It is not clear if this is due to a primary effect on the feeding system or a secondary improvement in the mental health of the patients. Many subjects who have had this operation were psychotic, and the frontal lobotomy was performed for therapeutic purposes. Cats, monkeys, and rats, however, also increase their food consumption following frontal lobotomy.[2, 44, 47] This operation also increases motor activity in lower animals, so the hyperphagia could be secondary to the increased activity level. Finally, as with damage to the hippocampus and septum, animals with a frontal lobotomy have difficulty suppressing responses, even when it is adaptive to do so. Their hyperphagia, therefore, might not reflect the disruption of a neural system concerned specifically with feeding behavior.

Midbrain

Electrolytic lesions of the midbrain reticular formation are followed by aphagia and adipsia,[13, 41] while electrical stimulation induces eating.[59] Simultaneous destruction of facilitatory and inhibitory systems at the midbrain level produces aphagic animals that turn into voracious eaters difficult to satiate, if food is placed in their mouths;[54] the absence of facilitatory structures results in an inability to start eating, and the absence of an inhibitory system results in a lack of satiety once eating begins.

More recent evidence suggests that the system of fibers connecting the substantia nigra and ventral tegmentum to the striatum in the telencephalon constitutes an important part of the feeding system. Electrolytic lesions of this neural substrate, as well as chemical ablation (using 6-hydroxydopamine) that interferes selectively with monoamine neurons, produce a syndrome of aphagia and adipsia very similar to the one observed after lesioning the lateral hypothalamus.[56]

BIBLIOGRAPHY

1. Anand, B. K., and Brobeck, J. R. Food intake and spontaneous activity of rats with lesions in the amygdaloid nuclei. *J. Neurophysiol.* 15 (1952): 421–430.

2. Anand, B. K.; Dua, S.; and Chhina, G. S. Higher nervous control over food intake. *Ind. J. Med. Res.* 46 (1958): 277–287.

3. Beatty, W. W., and Schwartzbaum, J. S. Commonality and specificity of behavioral dysfunctions following septal and hippocampal lesions in rats. *J. Comp. Physiol. Psychol.* 66 (1968): 60–68.

4. ———. Enhanced reactivity to quinine and saccharin solutions following septal lesions in the rat. *Psychon. Sci.* 8 (1967): 483–484.

5. Booth, D. A. Localization of the adrenergic feeding system in the rat diencephalon. *Science* 158 (1967): 515–517.

6. Coury, J. N. Neural correlates of food and water intake in the rat. *Science* 156 (1967): 1763–1765.

7. Donovick, P. J.; Burright, R. G.; and Helson, P. L. G. Body weight and food and water consumption in septal lesioned and operated control rats. *Psychol. Rep.* 25 (1969): 303–310.

8. Douglas, R. J. The hippocampus and behavior. *Psychol. Bull.* 67 (1967): 416–442.

9. Ehrlich, A. Effects of tegmental lesions on motivated behavior in rats. *J. Comp. Physiol. Psychol.* 56 (1963): 390–396.

10. Entingh, D. Perseverative responding and hyperphagia following Entorhinal lesions. *J. Comp. Physiol. Psychol.* 75 (1971): 50–58.

11. Fisher, A. E. The role of limbic structures in the central regulation of feeding and drinking behavior. In *Neural regulation of food and water intake. Ann. N. Y. Acad. Sci.* 157 (1968): 894–901.

12. Fonberg, E., and Delgado, J. M. R. Avoidance and alimentary reactions during amygdala stimulation. *J. Neurophysiol.* 24 (1961): 651–664.

13. Gold, R. M. Aphagia and adipsia following unilateral and bilateral asymmetrical lesions in rats. *Physiol. Behav.* 2 (1967): 211–220.

14. Graham, V. G. Functions of the amygdala. *Psychol. Bull.* 62 (1964): 89–109.

15. Grant, L. D., and Jarrard, L. E. Functional dissociation within hippocampus. *Brain Res.* 10 (1968): 392–401.

16. Green, J. D.; Clemente, C. D.; and deGroot, J. Rhinencephalic lesions and behavior in cats. Analysis of the Klüver–Bucy syndrome with particular reference to normal and abnormal sexual behavior. *J. Comp. Neurol.* 108 (1957): 505–536.

17. Grossman, S. P. Behavioral effects of chemical stimulation of the ventral amygdala. *J. Comp. Physiol. Psychol.* 57 (1964): 29–36.

18. ———. Effect of chemical stimulation of the septal area on motivation. *J. Comp. Physiol. Psychol.* 58 (1964): 194–200.

19. ———, and Grossman, L. Food and water intake following lesions or electrical stimulation of amygdala. *Amer. J. Physiol.* 205 (1963): 761–765.

20. Hecaen, H. Mental symptoms associated with tumors of the frontal lobe. In *The frontal granular cortex and behavior,* ed. J. M. Warren and K. Avert. New York: McGraw-Hill, 1964.

21. Hofstatter, L.; Smolik, E. A.; and Busch, A. K. Prefrontal lobotomy in treatment of chronic psychosis. *Arch. Neurol. Psychiat.* 53 (1945): 125–130.

22. Kaada, B. R. Somato-motor, autonomic and electrocorticographic responses to electrical stimulation of "Rhinencephalic" and other structures in primates, cat, and dog. *Acta. Physiol. Scand.* 24, Suppl. 83 (1951): 1–258.

23. ———; Pribram, K.; and Epstein, J. Respiratory and vascular responses in monkeys from temporal lobe, insula, orbital surface and cingulate gyrus. *J. Neurophysiol.* 12 (1949): 347–356.

24. Keesey, R. E., and Powley, T. L. Enhanced lateral hypothalamic reward sensitivity following septal lesions in the rat. *Physiol. Behav.* 3 (1968): 557–562.

25. Kling, A., and Hutt, T. J. Effect of hypothalamic lesions on the amygdala syndrome in the cat. *Arch. Neurol. Psychiat.* 79 (1958): 511–517.

26. Kling, A., and Schwartz, N. B. Effect of amygdalectomy on feeding in infant and adult animals. *Fed. Proc.* 20 (1961): 335.

27. Klüver, H., and Bucy, P. C. Preliminary analysis of functions of the temporal lobes in monkeys. *Arch. Neurol. Psychiat.* 42 (1939): 979–1000.

28. ———. "Psychic blindness" and other symptoms following bilateral temporal lobectomy in rhesus monkeys. *Amer. J. Physiol.* 119 (1937): 352–353.

29. Koikegami, H.; Fuse, S.; Yokoyama, T.; Watanabe, T.; and Watanabe, H. Contributions to the comparative anatomy of the amygdaloid nuclei of mammals with some experiments of their destruction or stimulation. *Folia. Psychiat. Neurol. Japon.* 8 (1955): 336–370.

30. Lubar, J. F., and Wolfe, J. W. Increased basal water intake and food ingestion in cingulectomized rats. *Psychon. Sci.* 1 (1964): 289–290.

31. MacLean, P. D., and Delgado, J. M. R. Electrical and chemical stimulation of fronto-temporal portions of limbic system in the waking animal. *EEG clin. Neurophysiol.* 5 (1953): 91–100.

32. Maire, F. W., and Patton, H. D. Eating and drinking responses elicited by diencephalic stimulation in unanesthetized rats. *Fed. Proc.* 15 (1956): 124 (No. 403).

33. McCleary, R. A. Response specificity in the behavioral effects of limbic system lesions in the cat. *J. Comp. Physiol. Psychol.* 54 (1961): 605–613.

34. Milgram, N. W. Effect of hippocampal stimulation on feeding in the rat. *Physiol. Behav.* 4 (1969): 665–670.

35. Morgane, P. J., and Kosman, A. J. Alterations in feline behavior following bilateral amygdalectomy. *Nature* 180 (1957): 598–600.

36. ———. A rhinencephalic feeding center in the cat. *Amer. J. Physiol.* 197 (1959): 158–162.

37. ———. Relationship of middle hypothalamus to amygdalar hyperphagia. *Amer. J. Physiol.* 198 (1960): 1315–1318.

38. Niki, H. The effects of hippocampal ablation on the behavior of the rat. *Jap. Psychol. Res.* 4 (1962): 139–153.

39. Obrador, A. S. Temporal lobotomy. *J. Neuropath. Exp. Neurol.* 6 (1947): 185–193.

40. Papez, J. W. A proposed mechanism of emotion. *Arch. Neurol. Psychiat.* 38 (1937): 725–743.

41. Parker, S. W., and Feldman, S. M. Effect of mesencephalic lesions on feeding behavior in rats. *Exp. Neurol.* 17 (1967): 313–326.

42. Pizzi, W. J. and Lorens, S. A. Effects of lesions in the amygdalo-hippocampo-septal system on food and water intake in the rat. *Psychon. Sci.* 7 (1967): 187–188.

43. Pribram, K. H., and Bagshaw, M. Further analysis of the temporal lobe syndrome utilizing fronto-temporal ablations. *J. Comp. Neurol.* 99 (1953): 347–375.

44. Richter, C. P., and Hawkes, C. D. Increased spontaneous activity and food intake produced in rats by removal of the frontal poles of the brain. *J. Neurol. Psychiat.* 2 (1939): 231–242.

45. Rioch, D. McK., and Brenner, C. Experiments on the corpus striatum and rhinencephalon. *J. Comp. Neurol.* 68 (1938): 491–507.

46. Robinson, B. W., and Mishkin, M. Alimentary responses evoked from forebrain structures in Macaca mulata. *Science* 136 (1962): 260–262.

47. Ruch, T. C., and Shenkin, H. A. The relation of area 13 on orbital surface of frontal lobes to hyperactivity and hyperphagia in monkeys. *J. Neurophysiol.* 6 (1943): 349–360.

48. Ruch, T. C.; Blum, M.; and Brobeck, J. R. Taste disturbances from thalamic lesions in monkeys. *Amer. J. Physiol.* 133 (1941): 433–434.

49. Sawa, M.; Yukiharu, U.; Masaya, A.; and Toshio, H. Preliminary report on the amygdalectomy on the psychotic patients, with interpretation

of oral-emotional manifestations in schizophrenics. *Folia. Psychiat. Neurol. Japon.* 7 (1954): 309–316.

50. Schreiner, L.; Rioch, D. McK.; Pechtel, C.; and Masserman, J. H. Behavioral changes following thalamic injury in cat. *J. Neurophysiol.* 16 (1953): 234–246.

51. Schwartzbaum, J. S. Some characteristics of "amygdaloid hyperphagia" in monkeys. *J. Psychol.* 74 (1961): 252–259.

52. Singh, D., and Meyer, D. R. Eating and drinking by rats with lesions of the septum and the ventromedial hypothalamus. *J. Comp. Physiol. Psychol.* 65 (1968): 163–166.

53. Smith, O. A.; MacFarland, W. L.; and Teitelbaum, H. Motivational concomitants of eating elicited by stimulation of the anterior thalamus. *J. Comp. Physiol. Psychol.* 54 (1961): 484–488.

54. Sprague, J. M.; Chambers, W. W.; and Stellar, E. Attentive, effective, and adaptive behavior in the cat. *Science* 133 (1961): 165–173.

55. Terzian, H., and Dalle Ore, G. Syndrome of Klüver and Bucy reproduced in man by bilateral removal of the temporal lobes. *Neurology* 5 (1955): 373–380.

56. Ungestedt, U. Adipsia and aphagia after 6-hydroxydopamine induced degeneration of the nigro-striatal dopamine system. *Acta Physiol. Scand.* 82, suppl. 567 (1971): 95–122.

57. White, N. M., and Fisher, A. E. Relationship between amygdala and hypothalamus in the control of eating behavior. *Physiol. Behav.* 4 (1969): 199–205.

58. Wood, C. D. Behavioral changes following discrete lesions of temporal lobe structures. *Neurology* 8 (1958): 215–220.

59. Wyrwicka, W., and Doty, R. W. Feeding induced by electrical stimulation of the brain stem. *Exp. Brain. Res.* 1 (1966): 152–160.

CHAPTER 5

Chemical and
Thermal Factors

While energy consumption varies somewhat from meal to meal, animals are quite accurate in the long-term regulation of their energy intake. They maintain a relatively constant body weight in relation to normal growth. Scientists have long been searching for the physiological mechanisms responsible for such regulation. It is clear that the organism must be sensitive to some correlates of energy depletion and some correlates of energy excess. At the same time, it must possess a model of normality, a set point around which it regulates and maintains its energy stores.

During the last 50 years, scientists have suggested 6 different feedback mechanisms by which the body's nutritive requirements could be signaled to the brain. The *humorstatic* theory states that certain hormones produced during hunger or satiety carry a message to the brain which results in an increase or decrease of feeding behavior. The *lipostatic* theory proposes that a lipid (fat) fraction provides the feedback information to the brain. The *aminostatic* theory emphasizes the role of amino acids, the building blocks for protein, as the critical regulatory chemical, while the *glucostatic* theory postulates that glucose is most important in the regulation of food intake. The *thermostatic* theory hypothesizes that animals regulate energy by means of some correlate of body temperature, and, most recently, a *neurohumoral* theory has been proposed.

Humorstatic Theory and Transfer Experiments

In a way, this has been the mother theory for the rest of the hypothesized mechanisms for controlling energy balance. One of the first successful experiments in this category was performed more than half a century ago by Luckhardt and Carlson.[82] These investigators took blood from the carotid artery in the neck of a starving dog, and injected it into the saphenous vein in the leg of a nondeprived dog. The injection heightened muscle tonus and contractions in the stomach and the dog increased its food intake. The authors concluded that the body tissues of a starved animal secrete a "hunger hormone" capable of inducing feeding behavior when injected into a satiated organism.

Nearly 60 years later the counterpart to this experiment was performed.[28] Starved rats, trained to consume their daily ration of food in a half hour period, reduced their intake by 50 percent following a transfusion into the jugular vein of the neck with blood withdrawn from the jugular vein of a satiated rat. However, eating behavior was not induced with a reversal of the procedure. It was concluded that the blood of an animal given free access to food contains a factor that inhibits eating. It is not clear, however, whether the failure to induce eating (as Luckhardt and Carlson accomplished with the dog) is due to the species difference or to the different vessels used in the transfer of the blood.

A more sophisticated method for producing exchange of blood factors between two animals is parabiosis,[36] a surgical procedure which unites two animals both anatomically and physiologically. The operation makes siamese twins out of two independent and separate organisms. After the animals have been surgically united, a network of small blood vessels is established between them at the point where their skin has healed together. The efficiency of the parabiosis depends on the extent and efficiency of the vascular bed shared by the tissues of the two animals. Figure 5–1 provides an example of a parabiotic preparation in which one member has been made diabetic by chemically destroying the insulin producing cells of the pancreas with alloxan. However, the severity of its diabetes is greatly reduced because insulin is available from its partner. If the partners are separated, the diabetic member soon dies; if insulin is injected into only one member of a diabetic pair, the blood sugar is reduced in both. Insulin crosses the parabiotic junction, demonstrating a functional interconnection between a parabiotic pair.

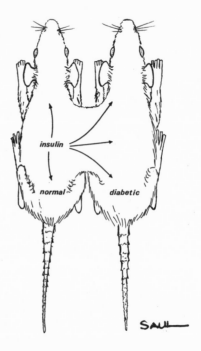

Figure 5–1. Dorsal view of a parabiotic preparation. The animal on the right has been made diabetic; however, the insulin secreted by the animal on the left is sufficient to maintain both members alive.

Parabiotic animals have provided a useful preparation for testing the humorstatic theory. In one of the initial studies of this preparation, Hervey united a parabiotic pair of rats at 25 days of age.[56, 57] The pair was permitted free access to food and water until reaching adulthood, at which time bilateral ventromedial hypothalamic lesions were made in one of the animals. The animal subjected to the hypothalamic lesion became hyperphagic and obese, while his parabiotic partner lost weight. Food intake was not measured in these early experiments, but visual observation left no doubt that the lesioned animals were hyperphagic. Their body fat was four times that of a normal rat.

Hervey also found that the nonlesioned partners of the parabiotic pairs ate less than normal rats. Their intestines contained very little food—less than that found in normal animals or parabiotic animals without lesions. Their body fat was less than 20 percent of normal. The investigator concluded that some blood-borne factor which inhibits food intake was produced in the obese member and reduced food intake in its partner.

The parabiotic animals with hypothalamic lesions ate even more than would normally be expected following damage to the ventromedial nucleus. It is possible that the underfed member of a parabiotic pair produces a humoral agent which increases food intake in its lesioned partner beyond that ordinarily seen in the hyperphagia resulting from lesions in the ventromedial nucleus.

Other experimenters, using similar parabiotic preparations with hypothalamic lesions, have been unsuccessful in replicating some of the original findings. When a parabiotic pair is forced to consume all their daily food within a 10-hour period, the ventromedially lesioned animal becomes hyperphagic, but its partner does not decrease food intake.[38, 52] It is known, however, that changing the pattern of meals by restricting access to the food supply leads to increased fat deposits. This could account for the evident lack of hypophagia and the normal fat content in the non-lesioned member of the parabiotic pair. That is, even though an inhibitory factor may circulate in the blood, its effect might be counteracted by the feeding schedule forced upon the animals.

More recent work strongly supports the idea that there is an appetite suppressing factor which can cross the parabiotic barrier.[38] Pairs of normal parabiotic rats were trained to eat their daily food intake within a 3-hour period. The animals were placed in a specially designed cage that partially separated them and permitted measurement of individual food consumption. When 1 member of the pair was allowed to start eating 2 hours before the other, the 3-hour food intake of the second rat decreased significantly. If shorter intervals were used between the meals of the first and second members of the pair, no such inhibition was observed. Apparently there is a satiety invoking factor, very likely non-neural, which requires about 3 hours to exert its suppressing effect on food intake.

The direct transfer of material from 1 brain to another also demonstrates the presence of some chemical factor released during a state of hunger.[97, 98] Monkeys were implanted with a special type of push-pull cannula which permits simultaneous injection and withdrawal of liquid from the brain or 1 of its ventricles. When the cerebrospinal fluid of 1 monkey, which has been deprived of food, is transfused into the lateral hypothalamus of a sated monkey, the recipient monkey begins to eat within minutes. Similar results are obtained if the transfused fluid is obtained by washing the lateral hypothalamus of a deprived donor with saline and injecting the perfusate into the lateral hypothalamus of the recipient. Whatever the substance released during a state of hunger, it must be present in the lateral hypothalamus as well as in the cerebrospinal fluid. Whether the substance is produced at these 2 sites or travels there from elsewhere is not known. It could be a peripheral chemical capable of crossing the brain blood barrier, or it could be produced in the brain. It is sufficiently stable to last in an active form for several minutes, the time necessary to complete the transfusion.

These transfer experiments were concerned with demonstrating the presence of an unspecified "blood factor" rather than with the nature of the factor itself. The following theories are more specific in scope. However, they share with the humorstatic theory assumption of a feedback mechanism whereby some humoral agent influences the brain's control over food intake.

Lipostatic Theory

According to this theory, energy balance is accomplished by monitoring and regulating the existing amounts of fat in the organism. Kennedy has been the main proponent of lipostatic control of food intake and energy regulation, based on his extensive work with ventromedial lesions during the last 3 decades.[71, 72, 73] According to him, the increase in weight in these animals is totally accounted for by excessive fat deposits, and the hyperphagia remains only until a certain amount of fat is deposited. The feeding behavior of the animals then returns to normal, although now regulated at this new level. Starvation and reduction of fat deposits is followed immediately by the return of hyperphagia, until the previous level of obesity is reached. Many workers agree that the ventromedial lesioned animal develops a new and higher set point for regulation of body weight or some correlate of body weight, such as fat deposits.[27, 62]

Feeding behavior is greatly influenced by body weight. Modifications of body weight not only affect the abnormal feeding responses following hypothalamic lesions, but the eating of normal animals as well. If normal animals are force-fed until they become obese, or partially food deprived until they become lean, the resulting feeding behavior depends on their body weight. Obese animals greatly reduce their food intake until they reach normal weight, while lean animals overeat for the same purpose. If animals are made obese by daily injections of insulin and then ventromedially lesioned, the subsequent hyperphagia is greatly reduced; often it does not appear at all.[62] These experiments make it clear that the brain is sensitive to some correlate of body weight, and that the signal varies as the fat deposits vary. There is even evidence that the brain itself can directly modify peripheral fat deposits through the autonomic nervous system or the blood stream.

Which lipid factor or factors might be involved in the control of eating behavior is not known. There is some scant and indirect evidence to suggest a correlation between levels of circulating free fatty acids and total body fat.[14] At the same time, feelings of hunger or satiety also correlate somewhat with blood levels of free fatty acids.[64]

Perhaps the best evidence for lipostatic regulation comes from a study employing mice and a unique method of damaging the ventromedial nucleus. Rather than using electrolytic current to produce the lesion, Liebelt and co-workers injected gold-thioglucose (GTG), a substance that specifically concentrates in the ventromedial hypothalamic nucleus and destroys its cells.[77] These mice show the same stages of hyperphagia as do those animals receiving electrolytic lesions. After 20 to 60 days of dynamic hyperphagia and body weight gain, they resume almost normal eating but remain obese. Larger doses of GTG, resulting in more extensive ventromedial damage, lead to greater obesity.[77, 93] When starved, they lose weight, indicating no gross impairment of lipolytic processes, but again become hyperphagic and obese when food is available.[43]

The great increase in body weight in these mice is due mainly to an increase in their fat deposits. The inguinal fat deposit in the groins, which constitutes 6 percent of the intact animal's total fat, enlarges to constitute 7 percent. In the normal animal, fat deposits in the area of the gonads contain approximately 15 percent of the total fat; after the lesion they contain 25 percent.[78]

An equilibrium appears to exist between the different sites of fat deposit. If the gonadal fat of an obese animal is surgically excised, a further increase develops in the fat content of the inguinal area, and the mice increase their food intake.[78] Reduction in the body lipid mass, either by starvation or surgical removal, results in an increase in food intake in an attempt to restore body weight and body lipid content.

While overeating results in the accumulation of fat within fat cells, under certain circumstances it may also increase the number of fat cells.[60, 61] For example, a rat litter normally consists of about 12 to 15 pups, and the mother usually has sufficient milk to provide for most of them. However, if the litter size is artificially reduced to 4 pups, more milk is available to each, and they grow heavier than they normally would. Analysis of the fat content of these overnourished animals at time of weaning reveals that their obesity, which extends to adulthood, is mainly due to an increase in the number of their fat cells, although there is also some increase in the fat content of each cell.[74] This example of environmentally caused obesity demonstrates that the number of fat cells in an organism are not necessarily determined genetically. If this is also true in humans, it suggests that the occurrence of obesity in the adult human might be reduced by manipulating the infant's diet. It also suggests changes in the attitude toward persons with obesity due to an excessive number of fat cells, and their frequent complaint of intense hunger. If the intensity of hunger signals to the brain were somehow correlated with number of fat cells, depletion of fat during dieting would generate a stronger hunger signal than would occur in persons with obesity due to excessive deposits of fat in an otherwise numerically normal fat cell population. The psychological and medical management would vary greatly, depending on the patient's type of obesity.

A lipostatic control of energy regulation and food intake has considerable appeal. Lipoid tissue provides storage for great amounts of energy which are easily retrievable when the need for energy increases. Although the brain itself is unable to make rapid and efficient use of the energy stored as fat, the rest of the body is able to do so. Fat deposits and their metabolic turnover provide a buffer zone for drastic changes in energy requirements. Energy stored in the form of carbohydrates, by contrast, is easily and rapidly available to the brain as well as to the rest of the organism. It contains, however, only a fraction of the energy stored in fats. If we were to depend solely on energy from carbohydrates, we could not afford prolonged exercise or fasting periods between meals, both of which require more energy than can be stored in the form of carbohydrates.

Aminostatic Theory

Proteins and their elementary building blocks, the amino acids, are important components of all living tissue. Although some amino acids can be synthesized by the organism, the "essential" amino acids cannot be. These must be obtained from foodstuffs and are indispensable components of life.[104,148] From these facts, as well as from other experimental data,[3,40] Mellinkoff formally postulated an aminostatic regulation of food intake.[94,95] He found that an increase in serum amino acid concentration correlated with a decrease in appetite, while a decrease in serum amino acid concentration correlated with an increase in appetite. Since there are many conditions in which this correlation does not occur, as with the diseases hepatitis and diabetes, the initial hypothesis was modified to emphasize the pattern of blood amino acids rather than their concentration. It was assumed that the pattern of amino acids available to the cells would in some way influence not only their use, but also the animal's desire for food.

It appears that the amino acids may indeed exert some control over food intake. The mechanism is different from other metabolic regulatory theories in that it is not the absolute value or a utilization value which controls feeding, but the relation among the various essential amino acids available to the cells. Deficiency in one essential amino acid is sufficient to produce a decrease in feeding behavior, and replacement of the deficient amino acid leads to reinstatement of food intake.[40] In many respects, the proposed amino acid regulation of feeding behavior appears closely related to specific hunger mechanisms, and will be considered as such in Chapter 7.

Glucostatic Theory

Interest in glucose as the nutrient which controls eating behavior arose because of an early twentieth century belief that stomach contractions signaled hunger. This was the proposal of 2 pioneers in the field, Cannon [24] and Carlson.[25] It was later discovered that intravenous injections of glucose suppress stomach contractions, while insulin reduces blood glucose and increases stomach contractions.[22] These and other findings [107] made it logical to suspect that the control mechanism for eating was specifically sensitive to the level of blood glucose.

It was not until the 1950s that the first glucostatic theory of food intake and energy regulation was stated by Mayer.[88, 89] He proposed that glucose utilization rather than the absolute level of blood glucose was crucial, and that the site for glucose analysis and information processing lay in the central nervous system, specifically in the medial hypothalamic region. Mayer's theory generated more research than all the other theories about feeding considered together.

That glucose could be important in the control of food intake is suggested by several facts. First, the brain is very dependent on the availability of glucose. Moreover, carbohydrates are not stored in any appreciable amounts. Carbohydrate storage in an adult human, for example, provides only about 300 Kcal. It is far easier to decrease carbohydrate energy in a short time than to reduce the energy derived from fats or proteins. Carbohydrates also play an important role in the metabolic use of fats and proteins.

Many hormones have some influence on carbohydrate metabolism and, accordingly, the effect of hormones on glucose and eating has been widely studied. Two hormones in particular have been considered as central to glucose metabolism: insulin and glucagon. Both of these hormones are produced in the pancreas, in the islets of Langerhans. Insulin is secreted by the β-cells, glucagon by the α-cells.

Administration of crystalline insulin produces hypoglycemia, a lowering of blood sugar, for 1 to 2 hours. The injected insulin is rapidly removed from circulation, with a half-time of about 30 minutes. By facilitating the entry of glucose and amino acids into the cells, insulin plays a key metabolic role following the ingestion of food. It is required for the synthesis of such energy sources as glycogen and the triglycerides. Insulin also stimulates the uptake of glucose in both the liver and the muscles, and aids the metabolism of glucose in many other tissues.

Administration of glucagon, by contrast, elevates the level of blood sugar, a condition called hyperglycemia. During fasting, glucagon levels increase in response to the decrease in blood sugar. Glucagon secretion is also increased after injections of insulin. Its main effect is to convert the liver's glycogen, a starchlike substance, into usable glucose. It does not have a similar effect on the glycogen stored in muscles. Glucagon also breaks down fat deposits and releases free fatty acids. The main action of glucagon is to increase the level of glucose in the blood when its level decreases below a physiological set point.

It is now known that administration of insulin results in an increase of gastric contractions,[45, 110, 122] an effect which can be reversed by the administration of glucose.[9, 96] It appears that insulin does not act directly upon the stomach but on the nervous system, since its stimulating effect on stomach contractions disappears following section of the vagus nerve, which innervates the stomach.[109]

In addition to its effect on stomach contraction, insulin increases food intake in animals,[10, 84] including man.[65, 66, 127] The hunger inducing properties of insulin do not result from its peripheral gastric effects, since administration of insulin to humans with both vagus nerves cut was still followed by the sensation of hunger.[44] These studies do not, however, eliminate the peripheral action of insulin on the intestine as a contributor to hunger sensations.

While it was originally thought that the glucodynamic action of insulin occurs only in the periphery,[59] it has been shown more recently that insulin also has a direct action on the central nervous system.[29] Whatever its *modus operandi,* insulin does induce hyperphagia and changes in glucose utilization. Glucose utilization is measured as the arterio-venous glucose difference.[64, 65, 89] Small arterio-venous glucose differences correlate with hunger and increased food intake, while large arterio-venous glucose differences correlate with periods of not eating.[8, 88, 140]

Administration of glucagon, originally discovered as a contaminant of insulin, decreases gastric motility [139, 141] and gastric secretion [70, 81, 132] and counteracts the effects of insulin.[81] It also depresses food intake and hunger sensations of man and animals.[66, 106, 119, 123] Its behavioral effects seem to operate through the central nervous system. Glucagon is ineffectual in reducing gastric hunger contractions in animals with ventromedial hypothalamic lesions.[92]

The hyperglycemic action of glucagon is shared by another hormone, epinephrine, which is produced in the adrenal glands. The glucodynamic action of epinephrine differs from glucagon in that it can also induce glucose production from glycogen stored in muscle tissue. As would be expected, epinephrine is also a powerful depressant of feeding.[116, 117]

Animals are capable of responding hormonally to cues which signal an upcoming meal. While the evidence is indirect, it now seems likely that they can learn to secrete insulin or glucagon as a conditioned response.[11] For example, as we have seen, food intake increases after an injection of insulin. Following a series of daily injections of insulin, animals will respond with hyperphagia even after a saline injection. They respond as if they had been injected with insulin. This conditioned response is prevented by giving glucagon instead of saline, thus counteracting the conditioned hypoglycemia, or by repeating the daily saline injections until extinction of the conditioned response occurs.[10] The results of similar experiments—in which blood glucose rather than eating was monitored—also reveal a conditioned hypoglycemia,[4, 125, 149] although in some cases a compensatory, conditioned hyperglycemia has been obtained.[128]

The same kind of learning, but in the opposite direction, occurs with glucagon injections. Following a series of daily injections of glucagon, an injection of isotonic saline results in a conditioned response of hyperglycemia [10] which lasts for 3 days and then disappears. The depressed eating that follows glucagon injections can also be conditioned. An injection of saline, following daily doses of glucagon, delays the onset of the next meal. This effect also persists for about 3 days. Although these experiments did not measure insulin or glucagon directly, they point to an endogenous endocrine plasticity that probably reflects the action of these two hormones.

The depressant effect of epinephrine on food intake can also be conditioned.[116, 117] This suggests that other than pancreatic hormones may participate in the anticipatory reactions of the organism normally associated with feeding.

Measurement of the electrical activity of neurons in various parts of the nervous system lends some support to the glucostatic theory. Such activity has been measured following such manipulations as food deprivation, injection of insulin, food satiety, and intravascular glucose injections. During hunger caused by food deprivation or by injections of insulin, lateral hypothalamic neurons increase their activity, while ventromedial hypothalamic neurons decrease theirs. Conversely, during the sated state or following intravascular administration of glucose, ventromedial hypothalamic activity increases, while activity in the lateral hypothalamus is reduced.[5, 100, 102, 103]

More recently it has become possible, by means of electrophoretic methods, to inject minute amounts of glucose or other substances directly into hypothalamic neurons.[101] Not all cells respond to glucose, while some cells respond only to glucose. This lends support to the conception of a central glucose detection system. It is commonly thought that the lateral hypothalamic response to glucose is secondary to the changes produced by glucose in the ventromedial hypothalamus, but the experimental evidence does not warrant this conclusion.

Glucose injections also produce some changes in neuronal activity in the peripheral nervous system. Some have suggested the presence of a glucose detection system in the liver.[115] For example, following liver perfusions with glucose, the spike activity of the vagus nerve is greatly reduced.[99] This response is specific to glucose; even other sugars, at the same concentration, do not have the same effect.

There may be more than 1 glucoreceptor system. It is even

possible that glucoreceptors, at different sites in the body, meter glucose for different purposes. Liver glucose, for example, varies greatly between periods of eating and fasting. Brain glucose, on the other hand, remains relatively stable.

Since the 1949 discovery that obesity results from systemic injections of GTG,[17, 145] this substance has been used widely to study the role of glucose in the control of eating. It was first discovered that mice became obese after administration of GTG, and then it was found that GTG caused hypothalamic lesions.[32, 77] Other gold-thio- compounds, such as gold-thio-malate and gold-thio-galactose, had no such effect.[87, 91] It appeared that glucose was penetrating hypothalamic cells, carrying with it the poisonous gold radical. When sodium-thio-glucose is injected preceding the injection of GTG, there is neither hypothalamic damage nor obesity,[90] supporting the contention that the gold must be attached to glucose in order to penetrate the cell membranes. The prevention of GTG-induced lesions by sodium-thio-glucose is thought to be the result of competition for receptor sites in the hypothalamus.

Although some investigators believe the main site of GTG action to be in the ventromedial hypothalamic nuclei, others have reported diffuse lesions throughout the hypothalamus, especially along its basal part, as well as in the median eminence, the arcuate nuclei, and the medial aspects of the medial forebrain bundle.[32, 77, 87] Recently the concept of a specific site for glucose action, as measured by GTG-induced lesions, has been questioned. The fact remains, however, that following its administration, GTG spreads homogeneously throughout the brain, but causes lesions only in certain areas. This suggests that such areas must be especially sensitive to glucose and GTG. It is also known that many of the cells damaged by GTG are not neurons but special cells, neuroglia, lying in close contact with blood vessels.[83]

Ventromedial hypothalamic damage due to GTG can be modified by changes in glucose utilization.[29, 30] Intravenous injection of glucose before administration of GTG increases damage, by virtue of the fact that injection of glucose induces release of endogenous insulin. Administration of 2-deoxy-D-glucose (2DG), which inhibits glucose metabolism, prevents the occurrence of obesity in GTG-treated mice.[80] Diabetic mice with an insulin deficiency are resistant to GTG,[31] but a reversal of the diabetic condition, by injections of insulin, brings back the susceptibility to GTG. Injection of insulin directly into the hypothalamus of diabetic mice also restores their sensitivity to GTG.[29] This makes it clear that insulin can play an important regulatory role in some parts of the brain, contrary to what was once thought.[59]

Hypothalamic sensitivity to GTG varies, depending on the strain or species of the animal.[79] Mice, the most common species used for this research, are highly susceptible to GTG. Rats are so sensitive to GTG that most of them die after being injected with it. However, some experimenters have been able to reproduce in rats the GTG syndrome of mice.[33, 143]

As we have already seen, the rate at which the body cells are utilizing glucose, as measured by difference in amounts of arterial and venous glucose, correlated somewhat with whether or not the animal will eat. Depression of glucose utilization throughout the body by means of 2DG increases the feeding behavior of rats and monkeys.[131] Injection of 2DG into parts of the hypothalamus also can affect feeding behavior.[12] While placement of 2DG in the medial hypothalamus of satiated animals has no effect on feeding behavior, placement in the lateral hypothalamus induces eating. The effects of 2DG on hungry animals is reversed, with feeding increasing only when it is placed in the ventromedial hypothalamus. In some way not yet understood, the level of hunger or satiety appears to affect these two areas differentially in regard to their sensitivity to 2DG. In any event, 2DG probably competes with glucose for enzymatic sites in cells,[21, 133, 147] and some of these cells are probably glucoreceptors.

The effects of injecting glucose directly into the brain are uncertain. When placed into the brain ventricles, glucose sometimes reduces eating behavior,[54, 55] but sometimes it has no effect at all. The deposition of glucose into the hypothalamus can either increase feeding,[11, 12] or decrease it.[15]

Although the glucostatic theory has generated more research than has any other theory of feeding behavior, many experimental findings do not support it. While administration of glucose to hungry animals does reduce the amount they eat at a subsequent meal, some researchers believe that this effect is only secondary to peripheral, gastrointestinal changes, rather than to changes in the brain.[8, 66, 108] Others have found no effects at all of glucose on food intake.[67, 118, 129, 130] Although glucose is central to the glucostatic theory, it may be that administration of glucose is not sufficient to alter glucose utilization at the glucoreceptor sites. Modification of glucose utilization by either insulin or glucagon has proven to be more consonant with the theory, increasing and decreasing food intake, respectively. Sometimes, however, peak differences in glucose utilization do not correlate well with increased feeding.[68, 106] A more sensitive measure of glucose utilization than general arterio-venous differences might help to clarify such discrepancies. One would like to know more about glucose differentials between the blood supplies to different parts of the brain, or even between 2 populations of neurons.

Nevertheless, glucose remains a good candidate for the short-term regulation of food intake, while lipostatic processes regulate long-term energy balance. It is not known as yet whether an organism has separate carbohydrate and lipid control systems. It could be that there is only 1 system, with carbohydrates serving as a buffer for short-term oscillations and the lipid component providing regulation of long-term processes.

Thermostatic Theory

Since 1948, Brobeck has been the main proponent of this theory, which proposes that food intake is a mechanism of temperature regulation.[18, 19, 20] The idea is that animals eat to keep warm and stop eating to prevent hyperthermia or overheating. It is true that in many species,[34, 41, 42, 50, 124] including man,[69, 142] animals kept in low environmental temperatures (below 20°C) increase their food intake, and those kept in high environmental temperatures (around 30°C) reduce food intake. If given an opportunity, animals also compensate for changes in environmental temperature in other ways. They can use physiological responses such as piloerection,[144] shivering,[134] vasomotor reactions,[136] sweating,[13] or salivation.[49, 85] They can also protect themselves with behavioral responses, such as working in order to turn a heat lamp on or off,[120, 121, 146] working to get a cold shower,[35] building appropriate nests,[114] or increasing or decreasing locomotor activity.[113, 135]

Later refinements of the thermostatic theory propose that it is the specific dynamic action (SDA) of food which signals the intake of sufficient food and the necessity to stop eating.[111, 137] SDA refers to the amount of extra heat released during the process of food assimilation. When food is eaten, the organism puts out a certain amount of energy to break the foodstuffs down into smaller usable components. The result is an increase in oxygen consumption and body temperature. The digestion of protein, for example, can increase the body's metabolism by as much as 30 percent! According to the thermostatic theory, the satiety value of foods depends on their SDA. Since proteins have a higher SDA than do carbohydrates and lipids, meals rich in protein should result in satiety sooner than meals of carbohydrates or lipids. This has been verified. Animals adjust food intake in accordance to SDA rather than to changes in caloric value [138] (by bulk dilution or addition of fat). However, these facts must be considered with caution, since the reactivity of experimental subjects to taste factors was not considered. It is well known, for example, that animals prefer carbohydrate diets to protein diets, and prefer fat diets even more. This preference is not thought to relate to SDA, but to taste and textural factors.

Body temperature is controlled by systems located in the anterior hypothalamus and preoptic areas.[26, 39, 51, 53, 58, 85, 112] The use of specially designed probes which permit discrete cooling or warming of these areas strongly supports the thermostatic theory.[6, 7]

Local cooling of the preoptic and anterior hypothalamic areas results in an inhibition of water intake and an increase of food intake. Conversely, heating these same brain structures is followed by inhibition of food intake and facilitation of drinking behavior. This is the expected outcome if the thermostatic theory is correct. It is assumed that nerve impulses from these anterior centers are relayed to the feeding centers, thus modulating behavior.

Animals with lesions in the ventromedial hypothalamus compensate normally when submitted to either warm or cold environmental temperatures.[73] This happens whether the animals are in the dynamic or the static phase of hyperphagia. Since heat control is not impaired, it is clear that the ventromedial hypothalamus is not essential for the temperature modulation of feeding.

The SDA hypothesis alone does not satisfy the requirements of the thermostatic theory.[1, 2, 23, 105] Increases in body and brain temperature do not coincide exactly with the cessation of feeding and, moreover, they are influenced in part by the animal's obesity, and even by the temperature of the food ingested or the amount of chewing done. With our present amount of knowledge, thermostatic control of feeding remains only a possibility.

Neurohumoral Mediation

Whatever the nature of the feedback system that regulates food intake, it involves neural transmission of messages from one brain structure to another. This transmission appears to be channeled through a neural system highly sensitive to norepinephrine. While the neural system that controls feeding behavior is adrenergic,[47, 48] the system that mediates drinking behavior is cholinergic in nature.[37, 48] Deposition of norepinephrine in certain brain structures initiates feeding behavior, or potentiates ongoing feeding; [16, 46, 48, 97] in other structures it acts as an inhibitor of feeding behavior.[12, 75, 76, 86] Most of the structures already considered in the regulation of feeding are rich in adrenergic nerve fiber terminals. There is no evidence, however, that feeding regulation is mediated exclusively by adrenergic transmitters, or that adrenergic transmitters are involved only in control of feeding behavior.

No single theory satisfies all of the conditions necessary to predict feeding behavior and energy regulation. It is increasingly clear that regulatory systems in the animal kingdom are more complex than their counterparts in the engineering field. It is impossible to isolate one system in an organism without affecting other systems. Modifications of temperature, for example, change the work done by muscles and other effectors, altering glucose utilization, which in turn triggers a metabolic chain reaction that brings carbohydrate, lipid, and protein metabolic reactions into play. The different speed at which each system operates provides an orderly sequence, resulting in buffered, and not abrupt, interphases. Energy and metabolic changes that cannot be compensated for within the organism require incorporation of energy from the environment, usually by way of the primitive response of eating.

BIBLIOGRAPHY

1. Abrams, R., and Hammel, H. Hypothalamic temperature in unanesthetized albino rats during feeding and sleep. *Amer. J. Physiol.* 206 (1964): 641–646.
2. Adams, T. Hypothalamic temperature in the cat during feeding and sleep. *Science* 141 (1963): 932–933.
3. Almquist, H. J. Utilization of amino acids by chicks. *Arch. Biochem. Biophys.* 52 (1954): 197–202.
4. Alvarez-Buylla, R., and Carrasco-Zanini, J. A conditioned reflex which produces the hypoglycemic effect of insulin. *Acta Physiol. Latinoamer.* 10 (1960): 153–158.
5. Anand, B. K.; Chhina, G. S.; Sharma, K.; Dua, S.; and Singh, B. Activity of single neurons in hypothalamic feeding centers: effect of glucose. *Amer. J. Physiol.* 207 (1964): 1146–1154.
6. Andersson, B., and Larsson, B. Influence of local temperature changes in the preoptic area and rostral hypothalamus on the regulation of food and water intake. *Acta Physiol. Scand.* 52 (1961): 75–89.
7. Andersson, B.; Gale, C. C.; Sundsten, J. W. Effect of chronic central cooling on alimentation and thermoregulation. *Acta Physiol. Scand.* 55 (1962): 177–188.
8. Arteaga, A.; Valdivieso, V.; Valdes, R.; Torres, M. C.; and

Munoz, I. The relation between appetite and glucose arterio-venous difference. *Rev. Med. Chilena* 90 (1962): 592–596.

9. Aylett, P. Gastric emptying and change of blood glucose level as affected by glucagon and insulin. *Clin. Sci.* 22 (1962): 171–178.

10. Balagura, S. Conditioned glycemic responses in the control of food intake. *J. Comp. Physiol. Psychol.* 65 (1968): 30–32.

11. ———. Neurochemical regulation of food intake. In *The hypothalamus*, ed. L. Martini, M. Motta, and F. Fraschini, pp. 181–193. London: Academic Press, 1970.

12. ———, and Kanner, M. Specificity of medial and lateral hypothalamus to 2-deoxy-D-glucose and glucose: effects on feeding behavior. *Physiol. Behav.* 7 (1971): 251–255.

13. Beaton, L. E.; McKinley, W. A.; Berry, C. M.; Ranson, S. W. Localization of cerebral center activating heat-loss mechanisms in monkeys. *J. Neurophysiol.* 4 (1941): 478–485.

14. Bjorntorp, P.; Bergman, H.; Varnauskas, E.; and Lindholm, B. Lipid metabolization in relation to body composition in man. *Metabolism* 18 (1969): 120.

15. Booth, D. A. Effects of intrahypothalamic glucose injection on eating and drinking elicited by insulin. *J. Comp. Physiol. Psychol.* 65 (1968): 13–16.

16. ———. Localization of the adrenergic feeding system in the rat diencephalon. *Science* 158 (1967): 515–517.

17. Brecher, G., and Waxler, S. Obesity in albino mice due to single injections of goldthioglucose. *Proc. Soc. Exp. Biol. Med.* 70 (1949): 498.

18. Brobeck, J. R. Food and temperature. *Recent Progress in Hormone Research* 16 (1960): 439–459.

19. ———. Food intake as a mechanism of temperature regulation. *Yale J. Biol. Med.* 20 (1948): 545–552.

20. ———. Neural control of hunger, appetite, and satiety. *Yale J. Biol. Med.* 29 (1957): 565–575.

21. Brown, J. Effects of 2-deoxyglucose on carbohydrate metabolism: review of literature and studies in the rat. *Metabolism* 11 (1962): 1098–1112.

22. Bulatao, E., and Carlson, A. J. The relation of the blood sugar to the gastric hunger contractions. *Amer. J. Physiol.* 68 (1924): 148.

23. Burton, A. C., and Murlin, J. R. Human calorimetry. III. Temperature distribution, blood flow and heat storage in the body in basal conditions after injections of food. *J. Nutr.* 9 (1935): 281–300.

24. Cannon, W. B., and Washburn, A. L. An explanation of hunger. *Amer. J. Physiol.* 29 (1912): 444–454.

25. Carlson, A. J. The hunger contractions of the empty stomach during prolonged starvation. *Amer. J. Physiol.* 33 (1914): 95–118.

26. Clark, G.; Magoun, H. W.; and Randon, S. W. Hypothalamic regulation of body temperature. *J. Neurophysiol.* 2 (1939): 61–80.

27. Corbit, J. D., and Stellar, E. Palatability, food intake, and obesity in normal and hyperphagic rats. *J. Comp. Physiol. Psychol.* 58 (1964): 63–67.

28. Davis, J. D.; Gallagher, R. L.; and Ladove, R. Food intake controlled by a blood factor. *Science* 156 (1967): 1247–1248.

29. Debons, A. F.; Krimsky, I.; and From, A. A direct action of insulin on the hypothalamic satiety center. *Amer. J. Physiol.* 219 (1970): 938–943.

30. ———, and Cloutier, R. J. Rapid effects of insulin on the hypothalamic satiety center. *Amer. J. Physiol.* 217 (1969): 1114–1119.

31. ———, and Likuski, H. J. Gold thioglucose damage to the satiety center: inhibition in diabetes. *Amer. J. Physiol.* 214 (1968): 652–658.

32. Debons, A. F.; Silver, L.; Cronkite, E. P.; Johnson, H.; Brecher, G.; Fenzer, D.; and Schwartz, I. L. Localization of gold in mouse brain in relation to gold thioglucose obesity. *Amer. J. Physiol.* 202 (1962): 743–750.

33. Deter, R. L., and Liebelt, R. A. The development of acute gastric ulcers in rats treated with gold thioglucose. *Gastroenterology* 43 (1962): 575–584.

34. Durrer, J. L., and Hannon, J. P. Seasonal variations in caloric intake of dogs living in an arctic environment. *Amer. J. Physiol.* 202 (1962): 375–378.

35. Epstein, A. N., and Milestone, R. Showering as a coolant for rats exposed to heat. *Science* 160 (1968): 895–896.

36. Finerty, J. C. Parabiosis in physiological studies. *Physiol. Rev.* 32 (1952): 277–302.

37. Fisher, A., and Coury, J. N. Cholinergic tracing of a central neural circuit underlying the thirst drive. *Science* 138 (1962): 691–693.

38. Fleming, D. G. Food intake studies in parabiotic rats. *Ann. N. Y. Acad. Sci.* 157 (1969): 985–1002.

39. Frazier, C. H.; Alpers, B. J., and Lewy, F. H. The anatomical localization of the hypothalamic centre for the regulation of temperature. *Brain* 59 (1936): 122–129.

40. Frazier, L. E.; Wissler, R. W.; Stefler, C. H.; Woolridge, F. L.; and Cannon, P. R. Studies in amino acid utilization. I. The dietary utilization of mixtures of purified amino acids in protein-depleted adult albino rats. *J. Nutr.* 33 (1947): 65–83.

41. Fregly, M. J.; Marshall, W. B.; and Mayer, J. Effect of changes in ambient temperature on spontaneous activity, food intake and body weight of goldthioglucose obese and normal mice. *Amer. J. Physiol.* 188 (1957): 435–438.

42. Gasnier, A., and Mayer, A. Recherche sur la regulation de la nutrition. Part II. Mecanismes regulateurs de la nutrition chez le Lapin domestique. *Ann. Physiol. Physicochim. Biol.* 15 (1939): 157–185.

43. Gray, C. F., and Liebelt, R. A. Food intake studies in goldthioglucose obese CBA mice. *Texas Rep. Biol. Med.* 19 (1961): 80–88.

44. Grossman, M. I., and Stein, I. F. Vagotomy and hunger-producing action of insulin in man. *J. Appl. Physiol.* 1 (1948): 263–269.

45. ———; Cummings, G. M.; and Ivy, A. C. The effect of insulin on food intake after vagotomy and sympatectomy. *Amer. J. Physiol.* 149 (1947): 100–102.

46. Grossman, S. P. Behavioral effects of chemical stimulation of the ventral amygdala. *J. Comp. Physiol. Psychol.* 57 (1964): 29–36.

47. ———. Direct adrenergic and cholinergic stimulation of hypothalamic mechanisms. *Amer. J. Physiol.* 202 (1962): 875–882.

48. ———. Eating or drinking elicited by direct adrenergic or cholinergic stimulation of the hypothalamus. *Science* 132 (1960): 301–302.

49. Hainsworth, F. R. Saliva spreading, activity, and body temperature regulation in the rat. *Amer. J. Physiol.* 212 (1967): 1288–1292.

50. Hamilton, C. L. Interactions of food intake and temperature regulation in the rat. *J. Comp. Physiol. Psychol.* 56 (1963): 476–488.

51. Hammel, H. T.; Hardy, J. D.; and Fusco, M. M. Thermoregulatory responses to hypothalamic cooling in unanesthetized dogs. *Amer. J. Physiol.* 198 (1960): 481–486.

52. Han, P. W.; Mu, J. Y.; and Lepkovsky, S. Food intake of parabiotic rats. *Amer. J. Physiol.* 205 (1963): 1139–1143.

53. Hardy, J. D.; Hellon, R. F.; and Sutherland, K. Temperature-sensitive neurons in the dog's hypothalamus. *J. Physiol.* 175 (1964): 242–253.

54. Herberg, L. J. Hunger reduction produced by injecting glucose into the lateral ventricle of the rat. *Nature* 187 (1960): 245–246.

55. Herberg, L. J. Physiological drives investigated by means of injections into the cerebral ventricles of the rat. *Quart. J. exp. Psychol.* 14 (1962): 8–14.

56. Hervey, G. R. The effect of lesions in the hypothalamus in parabiotic rats. *J. Physiol.* 145 (1959): 336–352.

57. ———. Hypothalamic lesions in parabiotic rats. *J. Physiol.* 138 (1957): 15–16 P.

58. Hess, W. R. Hypothalamus und thalamus. *Experimentel Dokumente.* Stuttgart: Thieme, 1956.

59. Himwich, H. E.; Bowman, K. M.; Davy, C.; Fazwkas, J. F.; Wortis, J.; and Goldfarb, W. Cerebral blood flow and brain metabolism during insulin hypoglycemia. *Amer. J. Physiol.* 132 (1941): 640–647.

60. Hirsch, J., and Han, P. W. Cellularity of rat adipose tissue: effects of growth, starvation and obesity. *J. Lipid Research* 10 (1969): 77–82.

61. Hirsch, J.; Knittle, J. L.; and Salans, L. B. Cell lipid content and cell number in obese and nonobese human adipose tissue. *J. Clin. Invest.* 45 (1966): 1023.

62. Hoebel, B. G., and Teitelbaum, P. Weight regulation in normal and hypothalamic hyperphagic rats. *J. Comp. Physiol. Psychol.* 61 (1966): 189–193.

63. Holloway, S., and Stevenson, J. Effect of glucagon on food intake and weight gain in the young rat. *Canad. J. Physiol. Pharmacol.* 42 (1964): 867–872.

64. Itallie, van, T. B., and Hashim, S. A. Biochemical concomitants of hunger and satiety. *Amer. J. Clin. Nutr.* 8 (1960): 587.

65. Itallie, van, T. B.; Beaudoin, R.; and Mayer, J. Arteriovenous glucose differences metabolic hypoglycemia and food intake in man. *J. Clin. Nutr.* 1 (1953): 208–216.

66. Janowitz, H. D., and Grossman, M. I. Relation of blood sugar to spontaneous and insulin induced hunger sensations. *Amer. J. Physiol.* 155 (1948): 446.

67. ———, and Hanson, M. E. Effect of intravenously administrated glucose on food intake in the dog. *Amer. J. Physiol.* 156 (1949): 87–91.

68. Janowitz, H. D., and Ivy, A. C. Rate of blood-sugar levels in spontaneous and insulin-induced hunger in man. *J. Appl. Physiol.* 1 (1949): 643.

69. Johnson, R. E., and Kark, R. M. Environment and food intake in man. *Science* 105 (1947): 378–379.

70. Jow, E.; Webster, D. R.; and Skoryna, S. C. Effect of glucagon and insulin on gastric secretion in rats. *Gastroenterology* 38 (1960): 732–739.

71. Kennedy, G. C. Food intake, energy balance and growth. *Brit. Med. Bull.* 22 (1966): 216–220.

72. ———. The hypothalamic control of food intake in rats. *Proc. Roy. Soc. (London), B* 137 (1950): 535–548.

73. ———. The role of depot fat in the hypothalamic control of food intake in the rat. *Proc. Roy. Soc. (London), B* 140 (1952): 578–592.

74. Knittle, J., and Hirsch, J. Infantile nutrition as a determinant of adult adipose tissue metabolism and cellularity. *Clin. Res.* 15 (1967): 323.

75. Leibowitz, S. F. Reciprocal hunger-regulating circuits involving α- and β-adrenergic receptors located, respectively, in the ventromedial and lateral hypothalamus. *Proc. Nat. Acad. Sci. (USA)* 67 (1970): 1063.

76. Leibowitz, S. F., and Miller, N. E. Unexpected adrenergic effect of chlorpromazine: eating elicited by injection into rat hypothalamus. *Science* 165 (1969): 609–611.

77. Liebelt, R. A., and Perry, J. H. Hypothalamic lesions associated with goldthioglucose-induced obesity. *Proc. Soc. Exp. Biol. Med.* 95 (1957): 774–777.

78. Liebelt, R. A.; Schinoe, S.; and Nicholson, N. Regulatory influences of adipose tissue on food intake and body weight. *Ann. N. Y. Acad. Sci.* 131 (1965): 559–582.

79. Liebelt, R. A.; Sekiba, K.; Liebelt, A. G.; and Perry, J. H. Genetic susceptibility to goldthioglucose-induced obesity in mice. *Proc. Soc. Exp. Biol. Med.* 104 (1960): 689–692.

80. Likuski, H. J.; Debons, A. F.; and Cloutier, R. J. Inhibition of goldthioglucose induced hypothalamic obesity by glucose analogues. *Amer. J. Physiol.* 212 (1967): 669–676.

81. Lin, T. M.; Benslay, D. N.; Dinwiddie, W. G.; and Spray, G. F. Action of glucagon on gastric HCl secretion. *Fed. Proc.* 21 (1962): 265 Abst.

82. Luckhardt, A. B., and Carlson, A. J. Contributions to the physiology of the stomach. XVII: On the chemical control of the gastric hunger mechanism. *Amer. J. Physiol.* 36 (1915): 37–46.

83. Luse, S.; Harris, B.; and Stohr, R. P. Ultra-structural evidence for oligodendroglial transport of salt and glucose. *Anat. Rec.* 139 (1961): 250.

84. Mackay, E. M.; Callaway, J. W.; and Barnes, R. H. Hyperalimentation in normal animals produced by protamine insulin. *J. Nutr.* 20 (1940): 59–60.

85. Magoun, H. W.; Harrison, F.; Brobeck, J. R.; and Ranson, S. W. Activation of heat loss mechanisms by local heating of the brain. *J. Neurophysiol.* 1 (1938): 101–114.

86. Margules, D. L. Alpha-adrenergic receptors in hypothalamus for the suppression of feeding behavior by satiety. *J. Comp. Physiol. Psychol.* 73 (1970): 1–12.

87. Marshall, N. B.; Barrnett, R. J.; and Mayer, J. Hypothalamic lesions in goldthioglucose injected mice. *Proc. Soc. Exp. Biol. Med.* 90 (1955): 240–244.

88. Mayer, J. Glucostatic mechanisms of regulation of food intake. *New Engl. J. Med.* 249 (1953): 13–16.

89. ———. Regulation of energy intake and the body weight: the glucostatic theory and the lipostatic hypothesis. *Ann. N. Y. Acad. Sci.* 63 (1955): 15–43.

90. ———, and Marshall, N. B. Mode d'action de l'aurothio-glucose et regulation glucostatique de la nutrition. *C. R. Acad. Sci.* 242 (1956): 169.

Chemical and Thermal Factors

Chemical and Thermal Factors

91. ———. Specificity of gold-thio-glucose for ventromedial hypothalamic lesions and obesity. *Nature (London)*, 178 (1956): 1399–1400.

92. Mayer, J., and Sudsaneh, S. Mechanism of hypothalamic control of gastric contractions in the rat. *Amer. J. Physiol.* 197 (1959): 274–280.

93. McBurney, P. L.; Liebelt, R. A.; and Perry, J. H. Quantitative relationships between food intake, lipid deposition and hypothalamic damage in goldthioglucose obesity. *Texas Rep. Biol. Med.* 23 (1965): 737–752.

94. Mellinkoff, S. M. Digestive system. *Ann. Rev. Physiol.* 19 (1957): 193–196.

95. ———; Frankland, M.; Boyle, D.; and Greipel, M. Relation between serum amino acid concentration and fluctuations in appetite. *J. Appl. Physiol.* 8 (1956): 535–538.

96. Mulinos, M. G. The gastric hunger mechanism. IV: The influence of experimental alterations in blood sugar concentration on the gastric hunger contractions. *Amer. J. Physiol.* 104 (1933): 371–378.

97. Myers, R. D. Chemical mechanisms in the hypothalamus mediating eating and drinking in the monkey. *Ann. N. Y. Acad. Sci.* 157 (1969): 918–932.

98. ———. Transfusion of cerebrospinal fluid and tissue bound chemical factors between the brains of conscious monkeys: a new neurobiological assay. *Physiol. Behav.* 2 (1967): 373–377.

99. Niijima, A. Afferent impulse discharges from glucoreceptors in the liver of the guinea pig. *Ann. N. Y. Acad. Sci.* 157 (1969): 690–700.

100. Oomura, Y.; Kimura, K.; Ooyama, H.; Maeno, T.; Iki, M.; and Kuniyoshi, M. Reciprocal activities of the ventromedial and lateral hypothalamic areas of cats. *Science* 143 (1964): 484–485.

101. Oomura, Y.; Ono, T.; Ooyamo, H.; and Wayner, M. J. Glucose and osmosensitive neurons in the rat hypothalamus. *Nature (London)* 222 (1969): 282–284.

102. Oomura, Y.; Ooyama, H.; Yamamoto, T.; and Naka, F. Reciprocal relationship of the lateral and ventromedial hypothalamus in the regulation of food intake. *Physiol. Behav.* 2 (1967): 97–115.

103. Oomura, Y.; Ooyama, H.; Yamamoto, T.; Ono, T.; and Kobayashi, N. Behavior of hypothalamic unit activity during electrophoretic application of drugs. *Ann. N. Y. Acad. Sci.* 157 (1969): 642–689.

104. Osborne, T. B., and Mendel, L. B. Amino acids in nutrition and growth. *J. Biol. Chem.* 17 (1914): 325–349.

105. Passmore, R., and Ritchie, F. J. The specific dynamic action of food and the satiety mechanism. *Brit. J. Nutrition* 11 (1957): 79–84.

106. Penick, S. B., and Hinkle, L. E. Depression of food intake induced in healthy subjects by glucagon. *New England J. Med.* 264 (1961): 893–897.

107. Quigley, J. P. The role of the digestive tract in regulating the ingestion of food. *Ann. N. Y. Acad. Sci.* 63 (1955): 6–14.

108. ———, and Hallaran, W. R. The independence of spontaneous gastrointestinal motility and blood-sugar levels. *Amer. J. Physiol.* 100 (1932): 102–110.

109. Quigley, J. P., and Templeton, R. Action of insulin on the motility of the gastrointestinal tract. IV. Action on the stomach following double vagotomy. *Amer. J. Physiol.* 91 (1930): 482–487.

110. Quigley, J. P.; Johnson, V.; and Solomon, E. I. Action of insulin

on the motility of the gastro-intestinal tract. I: Action on the stomach of normal fasting man. *Amer. J. Physiol.* 90 (1929): 89–98.

111. Rampose, A. J., and Shirasu, M. E. Temperature changes in the rat in response to feeding. *Science* 144 (1964): 317–318.

112. Ranson, S. W. Regulation of body temperature. *Res. Publ. Ass. nerv. ment. Dis.* 20 (1940): 342–399.

113. Richter, C. P. A behavioristic study of the activity of the rat. *Comp. Psychol. Monograph* 1 (1922): 1–55.

114. ———. Total self-regulatory functions in animals and human beings. *Harvey Lectures* 38 (1942–43): 63–103.

115. Russek, M. Participation of hepatic glucoreceptors in the control of intake of food. *Nature (London)* 197 (1963):79–80.

116. ———, and Pina, S. Conditioning of adrenalin anorexia. *Nature (London)* 193 (1962): 1296–1297.

117. ———; Rodriguez-Zendejas, A. M.; and Pina, S. Hypothetical liver receptors and the anorexia caused by adrenaline and glucose. *Physiol. Behav.* 3 (1968): 249–257.

118. Russell, G. F. M., and Bruce, J. Capillary-venous differences in patients with disorders of appetite. *Clin. Sci.* 26 (1964): 157–163.

119. Salter, J. M. Metabolic effects of glucagon in the Wistar rat. *Amer. J. Clin. Nutr.* 8 (1960): 535–539.

120. Satinoff, E. Behavioral thermoregulation in response to local cooling of the rat brain. *Amer. J. Physiol.* 206 (1964): 1389–1394.

121. ———, and Rutstein, J. Behavioral thermoregulation in rats with anterior hypothalamic lesions. *J. Comp. Physiol. Psychol.* 71 (1970): 77–82.

122. Schapiro, H., and Woodward, E. R. The action of insulin hypoglycemia on the motility of the human gastrointestinal tract. *Amer. J. Digest. Dis.* 4 (1959): 787–791.

123. Schulman, J. L.; Carleton, J. L.; Whitney, G.; and Whitehorn, J. C. Effect of glucagon on food intake and body weight in man. *J. Appl. Physiol.* 11 (1957): 419–421.

124. Sealander, J. A. Food consumption in Peromyscus in relation to air temperature and previous thermal experience. *J. Mammalogy* 33 (1952): 206–218.

125. Segura, E. Insulin-like conditioned hypoglycemic response in dogs. *Acta Physiol. Latinoamer.* 12 (1962): 342–345.

126. Shipley, E. G., and Meyer, R. K. Diabetes in parabiotic rats. *Amer. J. Physiol.* 148 (1947): 185–192.

127. Short, J. J. Increasing weight with insulin. *J. Lab. Clin. Med.* 14 (1929): 330–335.

128. Siegel, S. Conditioning of insulin-induced glycemia. *J. Comp. Physiol. Psychol.* 78 (1972): 233–241.

129. Smith, M. H. Effects of intravenous injection on eating. *J. Comp. Physiol. Psychol.* 61 (1966): 11–14.

130. Smith, M. H., and Duffy, M. Some physiological factors that regulate eating behavior. *J. Comp. Physiol. Psychol.* 50 (1957): 601–608.

131. Smith, P., and Epstein, A. N. Increased feeding in response to decreased glucose utilization in the rat and monkey. *Amer. J. Physiol.* 217 (1969): 1083–1087.

132. Solomon, S. P., and Spiro, H. M. The effects of glucagon and glucose on the human stomach. *Amer. J. Digest. Dis.* 4 (1959): 775–786.

133. Sols, A., and Crane, R. K. Substrate specificity of brain hexokinase. *J. Biol. Chem.* 210 (1954): 581–595.

134. Spealman, C. R. A characteristic of human temperature regulation. *Proc. Soc. Exp. Biol. Med.* 60 (1945): 11–12.

135. Stevenson, J. A. F., and Rixon, R. H. Environmental temperature and deprivation of food and water on the spontaneous activity of rats. *Yale J. Biol. Med.* 29 (1957): 575–584.

136. Strom, G. Effect of hypothalamic cooling on cutaneous blood flow in the unanesthetized dog. *Acta Physiol. Scand.* 21 (1950): 271–277.

137. Strominger, J. L., and Brobeck, J. R. A mechanism of regulation of food intake. *Yale J. Biol. Med.* 25 (1953): 383–390.

138. ———; and Cort, R. L. Regulation of food intake in normal rats and in rats with hypothalamic hyperphagia. *Yale J. Biol. Med.* 26 (1953): 55–74.

139. Stunkard, A., and Plescia, A. D. The effect of IV administration of various nutrients on the hunger gastric contractions of a man with severe brain damage. *Amer. J. Clin. Nutrition.* 5 (1957): 203–211.

140. Stunkard, A. J., and Wolf, H. G. Studies on the physiology of hunger. I. The effect of IV administration of glucose on gastric hunger contractions in man. *J. Clin. Invest.* 35 (1956): 954–963.

141. Sudsaneh, S., and Mayer, J. Relation of metabolic events to gastric contractions in the rat. *Amer. J. Physiol.* 197 (1959): 269–273.

142. Swain, H. L.; Toth, F. M.; Consolazio, C. F.; Fitzpatrick, W. H.; Allen, D. I.; and Koehn, C. J. Food consumption of soldiers in a subarctic climate (Fort Churchill, Manitoba, Canada, 1947–1948). *J. Nutr.* 38 (1949): 63–72.

143. Wagner, J. W., and deGroot, J. Effect of goldthioglucose injections on survival, organ damage and obesity in the rat. *Proc. Soc. Exptl. Biol. Med.* 33 (1963): 112.

144. Walker, E. A., The hypothalamus and pilomotor regulation. *Proc. A. Res. Nerv. and Ment. Dis.* 20 (1940): 400–415.

145. Waxler, S., and Brecher, G. Obesity and food requirements in albino mice following administration of goldthioglucose. *Amer. J. Physiol.* 162 (1950): 428–433.

146. Weiss, B., and Laites, V. G. Behavioral thermoregulation. *Science* 133 (1961): 1338–1344.

147. Wick, A. N.; Drury, D. R.; Nakada, H. I.; and Wolfe, J. B. Localization of the primary metabolic block produced by 2-deoxyglucose. *J. Biol. Chem.* 224 (1957): 963–969.

148. Willcock, E. G., and Hopkins, F. G. The importance of individual amino acids in metabolism; observations on the effect of adding tryptophane to a dietary in which zein is the sole nitrogenous constituent. *J. Physiol. (London)* 35 (1906): 88–102.

149. Woods, S. C.; Makous, W.; and Hutton, R. A. Temporal parameters of conditioned hypoglycemia. *J. Comp. Physiol. Psychol.* 69 (1969): 301–307.

SUGGESTED SUPPLEMENTARY READINGS

Balagura, S. Hypothalamic factors in the control of eating behavior. *Adv. psychosom. Med.* 7 (1972): 25–48.

Brobeck, J. R. Neural regulation of food intake. *Ann. N. Y. Acad. Sci.* 63 (1955): 44–55.

Hoebel, B. G. Feeding: neural control of intake. *Ann. Rev. Physiol.* 33 (1971): 533–568.

Mayer, J. Regulation of energy intake and the body weight: the glucostatic theory and the lipostatic hypothesis. *Ann. N. Y. Acad. Sci.* 63 (1955): 15–42.

CHAPTER 6

Oropharyngeal and
Gastrointestinal Factors

The Chemical Senses

The chemical senses, gustation (taste) and olfaction (smell), play an important role in feeding. Based on the information gathered by these receptors, an animal proceeds to ingest or reject a particular foodstuff. By acting as a gating system, these senses contribute to the control of eating behavior. For example, if food is sufficiently adulterated with an unpalatable substance, such as bitter quinine, an animal will reject it,[61] even if the rejection leads to death by starvation. Conversely, if a substance is made highly palatable with a sweetening agent, an organism may eat excessive amounts of it [45] and thus create a positive energy balance. Neither of these responses is regulatory in terms of energy balance. Therefore, while the chemical senses are part of the feeding system, they are not always regulatory in function. As we shall see, however, some regulatory properties have been attributed to taste and olfaction.

Taste stimuli have been conventionally classified into 4 modalities: sweet, sour, bitter, and salty.[40] This may be an oversimplification, but attempts to classify taste qualities into other categories have proven ineffectual. When one introspects as to the flavor of a filet mignon, one's impression is not the result of a little bit of sweet, a little bit of sour, and so on, but rather a derivation from the interaction of oral (taste) and nasal (smell) chemoreceptors.[77]

It is even more difficult to classify odor stimuli. Existing classifications list great numbers of odor classes, e.g., floral, musky, or putrid.[40] A floral quality is less specific than a salty or a sour quality, which is usually perceived through the sense of taste.

The need for odor and taste classifications derives from the contention that there may exist in the receptor sites specific mechanisms sensitive to specific substances.[7, 34, 38, 78] It has been hypothesized, for example, that the majority of sweet substances have a common chemical structure to which a sweetness receptor is sensitive.[88] As in the case of the detection of chemicals circulating in the blood, no plausible explanation of the sensing mechanism has yet been given.

The detection and coding of a specific chemical stimulus may be accomplished by the organism in a variety of ways. Nearly 100 years ago, Johannes Müller proposed that the organism possesses various sensory channels which in themselves bias the perception of the real stimulus.[48, 84] The "place theory" of taste and olfaction, an extension of this doctrine, postulates the existence of specific sensory cells (in taste buds and olfactory buds) for each of the possible pure tastes and odors.[14, 15, 16]

In the case of olfaction, a substance is inhaled into the nose. A series of specialized structures inside the nasal cavity conduct the odorous substance toward the olfactory epithelium, where the olfactory receptors lie. Here the substance must form a solution with the moist environment before it can stimulate the receptors.

The tongue and oral mucosa, where the taste receptors are located, can be more readily examined, and more is known about their function. Various regions of the tongue are differentially sensitive to taste stimuli. The tip is mostly sensitive to sweet and salty, the basal part to bitter, and the sides to sour. However, electrophysiological recordings in single taste cells and fibers have shown that, although a taste receptor may be very sensitive to substances of one particular taste modality, it also responds to other flavors when their concentrations are increased.[62, 91] Thus, electrophysiological studies only partially confirm the place theory of taste. The same results have been obtained in studies of olfaction.[41]

A second theory, the "pattern" theory of taste and olfaction, hypothesizes that the basis for discrimination of flavors and odors is derived from the pattern of neural firing of a population of receptors.[44, 92, 94] Thus, if 2 substances produce similar neural firing patterns, they are perceived to be of similar taste.[37] Dissimilar discharge patterns mean that dissimilar flavors are perceived.

The nerves serving the chemical senses are not comprised of identical fibers, each producing a fixed pattern of firing for every different stimulus, nor are they comprised of single fibers, each responsive to a single stimulus. Some neurons may be grouped into classes according to the range of stimuli to which they respond, but many fibers possess unique response characteristics. Thus, the existing facts are compatible with both place and pattern theories of coding.

The Olfactory System

Following the activation of the receptor terminals, impulses enter the olfactory bulbs. Anatomical as well as electrophysiological studies suggest that considerable input integration occurs at this level.[1, 6, 28, 102] There is a convergence or funneling of fibers into a relatively small number of cells.[31, 32] These cells have been classified into 4 types, each one presumably having a different function. Various changes in the frequency and pattern of the original impulse occur at this level; [82, 83] then the neural information proceeds centrally by way of the olfactory tract and the anterior commissure.

Lesion degeneration studies have shown that, after lesions of the olfactory bulbs have been made, degeneration can be observed in many limbic structures.[24, 33, 75] If the olfactory bulbs are stimulated electrically, it is possible to detect alterations in neural activity throughout the limbic system.[3, 22, 105]

In a classical study, H. Swann, trained rats to discriminate between 2 odors (anise and creosote) in order to get a food reinforcement. After the subjects had reached a criterion of 90 correct responses out of 100, they were given electrolytic lesions in either the olfactory bulbs, the anterior commissure, the septum, the amygdaloid complex, the piriform lobes, or the hippocampus. Only in animals with lesions of the olfactory bulbs or of the anterior commissure was the olfactory threshold substantially increased.[19, 119, 120]

Other experimenters have found that amygdaloid lesions interfere with the learning of an olfactory discrimination, but not with its retention.[4] Studies of the frontal and temporal cortices have proven inconclusive as to the role these structures may play in olfaction.[5, 27]

The Gustatory System

The taste receptors are located in the taste buds found on the surface of the tongue and in the mucosa underlying the oropharyngeal cavity. Their numbers vary from 100,000 in the catfish to approximately 9,000 in man and only a few dozen in birds. Taste stimuli travel toward the brain by way of the facial, the glossopharyngeal, and the vagus nerves. The relative contribution to taste of each of these nerves varies with the phylogenetic level of the animal.

In mammals, the taste buds of the anterior two-thirds of the tongue relay gustatory information to the central nervous system by way of the lingual and chorda tympani nerves, both branches of the facial nerve (7th cranial). The taste receptors of the posterior third of the tongue are innervated by the glossopharyngeal nerve (9th cranial). The gustatory sensations of the pharynx and the larynx are mediated by the vagus nerve (10th cranial). The gustatory fibers from these nerves synapse at their respective levels of entrance in the medulla, then extend caudally in the fasciculus solitarius.[35, 93] After synapsing in the fasciculus, some fibers course toward the dorsal visceral gray, and from there to the thalamus and then the cerebral cortex. Other fibers, after entering the medulla, synapse in the ventral tegmental nuclei, and then travel to the hypothalamus. Degeneration studies, conducted after a lesion of the medial nucleus of the solitary tract, revealed degenerative changes in the lateral solitary nucleus, the nucleus of the vagus, and the dorsal reticular activating system.[81] These findings seem to indicate that gustatory signals are partially processed in the midbrain before they arrive at the thalamus.

The nuclei of the solitary tract have been shown to be involved in the behavioral system related to taste.[23] In an experiment, the rats' taste threshold for quinine was determined before and after lesions of the nuclei of the tractus solitarius. After surgery, thresholds increased by a factor of 30.

The thalamus is another important relay and integrational nucleus for taste sensations. Some cells in the ventral thalamus respond to gustatory, but not to thermal or mechanical, stimulation of the tongue.[17] Bilateral electrolytic lesions of the ventral thalamus are followed by a 20-fold increase over the preoperative rejection threshold for quinine solutions.[87]

Lesions of the cortical projection areas for taste have provided equivocal information. In one experiment an 8-fold increase in the taste threshold was found following cortical lesions,[18] but it is not clear whether it was secondary to the thalamic degeneration which followed the lesions. Results vary, depending on the testing or training paradigm: e.g., overlearning of a discrimination task prevents threshold changes following cortical damage.

Oropharyngeal Components of the Eating System

THE SATIETY EFFECT OF CHEWING AND SWALLOWING. Introduction of a food particle into the mouth is followed by a series of chewing movements that culminate in swallowing. During the execution of these movements, as the food is moved around in the oral cavity, its taste, smell, temperature, and mechanical and proprioceptive stimuli are continuously being relayed to the brain. Along with the sensory feedback from the act of swallowing, these stimuli are referred to as the oropharyngeal (mouth and throat) factors contributing to the control of food intake. All, or any number, of these stimuli can affect feeding behavior. To what extent one stimulus is more important than another is not known.

Science fiction writers have talked for many years of pill-size nutrients. According to them, 3 pills a day could provide man with all the required vitamins, energy, and protein necessary for growth and survival. Science is close to such an achievement, but people flinch at the thought of being deprived of tasting and chewing their food. For example, humans who cannot pass food through the esophagus for medical reasons, and have to be fed through a tube inserted into the stomach, ask for food to chew and taste while being fed through stomach tubes, even though they have to spit it out afterwards.

One of the first experiments separating the influence of oropharyngeal and gastrointestinal factors on feeding was performed a century ago by Claude Bernard.[21] He observed that if water were prevented from entering the stomach of a horse while it was drinking, the animal engaged in extremely long drinking bouts, followed by very short intervals of inactivity. This experiment clearly separated the oropharyngeal and gastrointestinal factors. The fact that the horse drank more than normal points to the role of stomach filling as a suppressant of drinking. That the horse stopped drinking at all indicates that oropharyngeal influences can have at least a temporary satiety effect. Bernard's method made use of an esophagostomy, as depicted for a human in Figure 6–1. The esophagus is severed at its lower third, and both ends are brought out to the skin. The animal is fed through the distal end, while whatever is swallowed comes out through the proximal end and thus fails to enter the stomach.

The chewing and swallowing of food also inhibits further

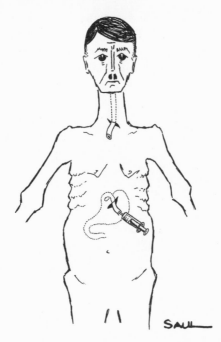

Figure 6–1. An esophagostomized human. Any material swallowed comes out through the proximal end of the esophagus; in order to feed the person, nutriments must be injected through its distal end.

intake, whether or not the food enters the stomach.[58] If a dog, for example, eats 3 times a day, his average meal is about 2.5 minutes long. After an esophagostomy, when no food enters the stomach, the same dog eats for 14 minutes. If the dog is then deprived of food for 18 hours and then offered food, he eats for 22 minutes. The animal does finally stop eating, and refuses food for an hour or so. The flavor of food plus the execution of chewing and swallowing movements exert a suppressant effect on further eating, and may even be rewarding, although no nourishment is received.

The importance of oropharyngeal factors has also been demonstrated by comparing the satiety value of normal eating with the satiety effect of placing food directly into the stomach. In one experiment, rats were trained to obtain their nutrients by pushing a small panel. All animals were deprived of food for 21 hours before each test. One group was permitted to drink 14 milliliters of a milk diet 10 minutes before testing. A second group was stomach loaded—the mouth was by-passed by means of a chronically implanted gastric tube (see Figure 6–2, top)—with 14 milliliters 10 minutes before testing. A third group was treated in the same

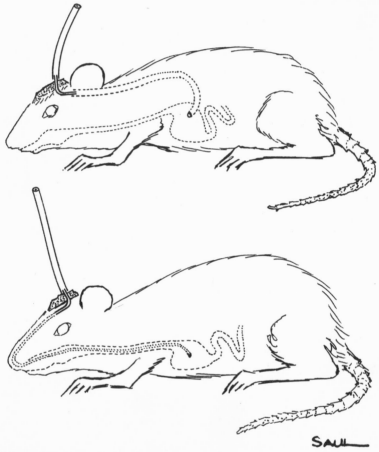

Figure 6–2. Two different ways of implanting a chronic nasogastric tube. *Top:* a rubber tube is placed under the skin of the back, then introduced into the stomach by piercing the stomach's wall. *Bottom:* a rubber tube is placed under the skin of the snout, then into the esophagus and the stomach. In both instances the other end of the tube is affixed to the skull with cement.

way as the second group, except that non-nutritive isotonic saline was injected into the stomach. The test simply measured the number of reinforcements (panel pushes) per unit of time obtained by each group 10 minutes after the initial manipulation. The animals permitted to drink prior to testing panel pushed at a slower rate and ate less than the animals stomach loaded with the diet; the latter, in turn, panel pushed and ate less than the saline loaded animals.[20, 63] Hungry animals will even learn to run a T-maze faster when they are allowed to swallow the food reward than when they are fed by stomach tube.[76]

THE ROLE OF TASTE AND SMELL. It is clear that animals

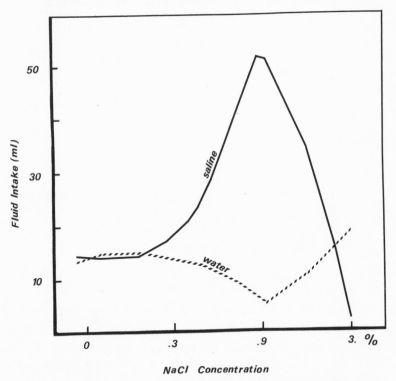

Figure 6–3. Results obtained in a 2-bottle test between water and various concentrations of saline. At low concentrations rats drink equal volumes of saline and water. However, rats seem to prefer a 0.9 percent saline solution over water, and water over a 3 percent saline solution.

use their chemical senses in selecting foodstuffs. The taste and olfactory properties of a substance are thus important in determining feeding behavior. Even when animals are presented with various concentrations of the same liquid substance, such as saline or glucose, they consume different amounts of each concentration, showing a relative preference-aversion curve, as depicted in Figure 6–3. It is known that this choice is dependent on taste, since cutting the taste nerves of the tongue causes equal amounts of the various concentrations to be consumed.[95, 103]

The same loss of preference also occurs when the mouth is

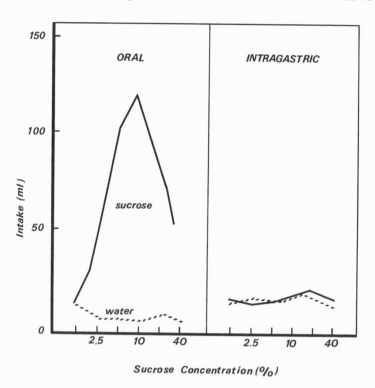

Figure 6–4. When rats are permitted to drink water or sucrose solutions, they show a clear preference for the latter. However, when they are fed through a gastric tube (as shown in Fig. 6–2, bottom), and are unable to taste the liquids, the preference for sucrose disappears. Adapted from K. T. Borer, *J. Comp. Physiol. Psychol.* 65 (1968): 213–221.

by-passed by feeding the animals through a tube directly into the stomach. Figure 6–4 compares the preference for sucrose solutions of various concentrations when ingested by way of the mouth or tubed directly into the stomach.[25, 26] The left side of the figure shows the daily intake of water and sucrose solutions when the animals ingested them through their mouths. As shown on the right side, the concentration preference disappears when the animals receive the solutions by way of a stomach tube.

Not only do animals have natural taste and odor preferences, they also can learn to discriminate between different foodstuffs on the basis of nutritional considerations. In one study, for example, rats were given the same basic diet with 2 different odors, designated as odor *A* and odor *B*. One group of rats, immediately after ingesting the *A*-odored food, received an additional load of glucose that added 25 percent more calories to the diet. A second group received the caloric supplement following ingestion of the food with odor *B*. The animals soon learned to decrease consumption of the odor-labeled diet supplemented with glucose, but ate the usual amounts of the other diet.[65] Rats learn the same type of adjustment if the diets differ in flavor rather than odor. When the hunger depressant amphetamine was mixed with one of the basic diets, learning also occurred. The diet supplemented with amphetamine was consumed in lesser quantities then the nonsupplemented diet. Furthermore, the animals were incapable of learning these discriminations if they were made anosmic (unable to smell) or given the same flavored food without a differential odor.[68]

Animals also learn to avoid certain foodstuffs on the basis of flavor. At the proper concentration, lithium chloride has a taste similar to sodium chloride, common salt. However, lithium chloride is a poison; if taken in sufficient amounts it can cause liver and kidney damage and even death. If thirsty rats are offered a dilute lithium solution, they will at first drink it and thus become sick. If, 5 days later, the survivors are made thirsty and again offered lithium to drink, they refuse it. Not only will they not drink the lithium solution, but they won't drink a similar tasting sodium chloride solution.[85] If, on the other hand, the lithium chloride is given by way of a stomach tube, thus eliminating taste, the survivors drink not only a sodium chloride solution, but a lithium chloride solution as well.[114] This mechanism, or a very similar one, is operating in the case of the bait-shy rodent.[106] Once rats ingest a poisoned food, they won't ingest it or similar food again. Thus the postingestional effects of many foodstuffs act to influence later taste preferences. Indeed, it is not always possible to get a clear picture of the primary role of the chemical senses if the ingested material is permitted to reach the stomach and have secondary physiological or pathological effects.

There is no doubt, however, that taste or palatability plays a substantial role in regulation of food intake. If rats are adapted to eating 4 meals made of the same basic foodstuffs, but of 4 different flavors, the daily intake is similar for all of the flavors. However, if at 1 meal period they are offered in succession all 4 flavors, the size of the meal increases substantially.[66, 67] The animals are not regulating energy input, but are consuming an excess of nutrients on the basis of palatability alone.

The importance of palatability in the food consumption of animals can be clearly demonstrated with saccharin. This chemical has a sweet taste when put in solution at a relatively low concentration, but it has no nutritive value. Consumption of this solution in preference to a nutritive substance is thus highly rewarding in terms of taste, but unwise in terms of nutritional regulation.[111] Nonetheless, many animals prefer saccharin to nutritive solutions of sucrose or glucose.[46] This does not seem to be a learned phenomenon since very young rats, given a choice among saccharin, lactose, and water, prefer saccharin.[54] Acceptance of different concentrations of saccharin varies with the state of deprivation of the organism. While maximum acceptance for a satiated rat occurs at a concentration of 0.4 percent, after food deprivation it increases to 3 percent. The animals respond to saccharin as they would to a nutritive solution, on the basis of taste alone.[9]

It is not possible, however, to fool an organism all the time merely on the basis of taste. Food-deprived animals given access to either nutritive 5 percent sucrose or 0.037 percent saccharin for 3 hours every day drank more saccharin than sucrose on the first day. On the following days, however, sucrose consumption increased 300 percent, while saccharin intake remained unchanged.[69] Although animals may initially prefer a substance on the basis of its taste or smell, a subsequent learned preference is greatly influenced by nutritional value.

It is difficult to separate the relative contributions of oropharyngeal and gastrointestinal feedback systems when an animal is fed sizable amounts of a substance. Esophagostomized animals with chronically implanted stomach tubes are now used to dissociate the contributions of these two systems. This type of surgical preparation permits an animal to ingest one solution, which passes out through the severed esophagus, while the experimenter injects the same or a different solution into its stomach. In this way the influence of the mouth and throat can be differentiated from that of the stomach.[79, 80]

The use of animals prepared in this manner has demonstrated clearly that the relative contributions of taste and feedback influences from the stomach vary greatly, depending on the combination of solutions being ingested and tubed into the stomach. As shown in Figure 6–5, when water is injected into a rat's stomach while it is offered water and various saline solutions, the rat's preference for dilute saline solutions disappears; the animal drinks equal amounts of the water and the hypotonic, isotonic, and hypertonic saline solutions. On the other hand, when saline rather than water is injected into the stomach, the animal consumes exaggerated amounts of water as well as of dilute solutions, and very little of highly concentrated solutions. Taste factors apparently have very little influence on the normal preference for dilute saline solutions, and perhaps play an inhibitory role in the case of hypertonic solutions.

If sweet solutions are presented to the animal while water is being injected into its stomach, a different picture emerges, especially in the case of sucrose solutions.[79] As the concentration in-

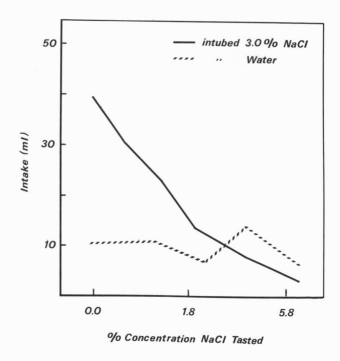

Figure 6–5. These data illustrate the fact that postingestional factors greatly influence the rat's preference and consumption of flavored solutions. When a hypertonic, 3.0 percent saline solution is injected directly into the stomach while the animal is offered various concentrations of saline, it shows a preference for water and for dilute solutions. This preference disappears, however, if water instead of concentrated saline is intubed into the stomach. Adapted from D. G. Mook, *J. Comp. Physiol. Psychol.* 56 (1963): 645–659.

creases, intake increases. The consumption of sweet solutions is greatly influenced by taste.

Gastrointestinal Factors

After a foodstuff is swallowed, it enters the gastrointestinal system. We will now consider this system's influences on hunger and satiety. The hormonal and chemical changes that occur after food has been absorbed from the gastrointestinal tract already have been considered in Chapter 5.

INITIATION OF EATING. While the need for nourishment is signaled to the brain by a number of physiological systems, man has always localized the sensation of hunger in the abdominal cavity, specifically in its upper portion below the ribs. Scientific papers on this matter were published as early as the eighteenth century. However, it was the work of Cannon and Carlson, during the first quarter of the twentieth century,[29, 30] that ushered in modern-day interest in this phenomenon.[50, 51, 58, 89, 110]

Washburn, one of Cannon's students, after fasting for a day, swallowed a deflated balloon attached to a rubber catheter. When the balloon reached Washburn's stomach it was inflated, and changes of pressure brought about by stomach contractions were recorded. Strong gastric contractions invariably preceded the sensation of hunger. The reflex contractions of the empty stomach were postulated to be the direct cause of the sensation of hunger.[29]

MOTOR COMPONENT. A gastric hunger contraction of the muscular wall of the stomach consists of what is known as a peristaltic wave. These contractions are from 30 to 120 seconds in duration and travel from the gastric fundus above to the corpus and antrus of the stomach below, and terminate in the duodenum.[97] Depending on the food-deprivation state of the organism, these contraction waves may follow one after the other. In man, following a 24-hour fast, sets of hunger contractions occur every one and one-half hours, and may last for 30 minutes. They occur more often, following a prolonged fasting period, and the periods of activity can be even more extended. The basic rhythm of these contractions is 3 waves a second. The waves can be classified into types I, II, and III, depending on the magnitude of their pressure. It is believed that true hunger pangs result from a periodic augmentation of type II waves, occurring at the basic rhythm of 3 a second.

It is well known that hunger contractions can be potentiated by food deprivation.[71] As deprivation continues, they grow stronger and more prolonged, reaching, in extreme cases, a continuous state of contraction known as tetany. Insulin, a hormone that induces eating, also increases gastric motility.[70, 99] This effect can be temporarily reversed by intravenous administration of glucose. Conversely, glucagon, a hormone that reduces appetite, decreases the hunger contractions induced by either food deprivation or insulin injections.[47, 116, 118] Somewhat surprisingly, no correlation has been found between hunger contractions and blood glucose levels.[70, 98] During fasting, when gastric motility is increased, glucose levels are often within the normal range.[97, 108] This is in accord with the fact that administration of glucose to fasting subjects fails to decrease subsequent eating.[56]

Gastric hunger contractions can also be influenced by electrical stimulation of the brain. As early as the 1930s it was known that electrical stimulation of the anterior hypothalamus increased gastric motility, while stimulation of the posterior hypothalamus led to decreased motility.[13, 73] Gastric contractions can also be increased by stimulating the lateral hypothalamus.[64] This latter effect is suppressed when both vagus nerves to the stomach are sectioned. By contrast, gastric motility is inhibited after stimulation of the ventromedial hypothalamus. Sectioning of the vagus does not reduce this induced inhibition, although excision of the celiac ganglia, in the abdominal cavity, does. Gastric motility is not completely dependent on neural connections, however, since it persists even if all nerves to the stomach are cut.[101, 104]

Experiments using the Heidenhain pouch preparation have shed further light on the mechanisms of gastric function. As shown in Figure 6–6, this preparation consists basically of an organism with 2 separate stomachs, one continuous with the mouth and esophagus, the other, the Heidenhain pouch, detached from the digestive tract. These stomachs can be made to share the same blood supply, or to have their own. Sometimes they are denervated by cutting all the stomach nerves.

The correlation between the contractions of the stomach and the pouch varies, depending on the experimental circumstances. For example, the spontaneous activity of the separated pouch

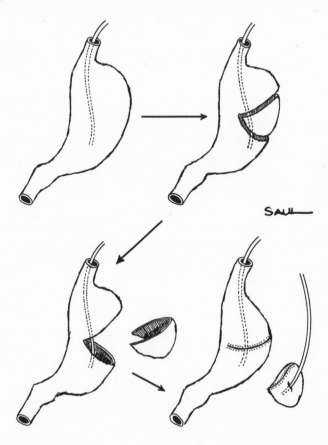

Figure 6–6. The basic surgical steps to make a Heidenhain pouch. The normal stomach is shown at top left. A piece of stomach is resected (top right, bottom left), then both the remaining stomach and the resected piece are sutured, and tubes placed in them to permit recording of their secretions and motility (bottom right).

can resemble that of the stomach, whether or not they are denervated,[104] because of the secretion of the intestinal hormone, enterogastrone, which inhibits motility in both stomach and pouch.[36] On the other hand, placing food in the stomach inhibits activity in the pouch only if the vagus nerve is intact.[104] Administration of insulin also increases both pouch and stomach motility only if the vagal connections have not been disrupted.[100,121] It is clear that gastric motility depends both on blood factors and neural factors.

The stomach is not necessary for eating to occur. When rats have their stomachs removed and the food passes directly into the intestines, they still eat enough to keep themselves alive.[122] The energy balance of humans who have had their stomachs surgically removed also remains unimpaired, although their feeding patterns are totally altered—they take very small meals several times a day.[52,72] Patients who have had all the nerves to the stomach sectioned continue to report feelings of hunger, although these feelings differ from normal in that no abdominal hunger pangs are felt.[43] Thus, while sensations from the stomach are an important cue in the feeling of hunger, their absence does not eradicate hunger sensations or the regulation of energy balance. At the same time, the absence of stomach cues does alter the schedule of food intake.

DISTENTION AND CALORIES AS SATIETY FACTORS. After a certain amount of food is taken into the stomach, further voluntary intake is reduced through the inhibitory effects of increased pressure within the stomach and the stretching of the stomach wall, as well as through the inhibitory action of the caloric properties of the food. Rats, for example, will learn to run through a maze correctly when their only reward is to have liquid food pumped directly into their stomachs.[76]

The inhibitory effects of gastric distention can be induced by either nutritive or non-nutritive substances.[60,109] While the combination of bulk and nutrients in the stomach is the most effective way to induce satiation, even the inflation of a balloon within the stomach can produce this effect. However, the distention by balloon necessary to induce a cessation of eating is far greater than that required from a normal meal.

Distention of the intestines also contributes to the cessation of eating. When human subjects ingest as much of a non-nutritive liquid as they can, X-rays reveal that, at the time they feel full, the upper intestine is more distended than the stomach.[49] This seems equally true in rats. For example, immediately following intragastric loads of 6, 12, or 25 milliliters, the abdomens were cut open and the amount of liquid in their stomachs was measured.[12] At the same time, the length of that part of the intestines filled with the liquid was determined. Most of the 6-milliliter load remained in the stomach, but only about 7 milliliters of the 12- or 25-milliliter loads remained in the gastric cavity, the rest having filled the intestinal tube up to the colon. It is interesting to note that, under certain circumstances, rats will voluntarily drink as much as or more than these quantities.

Different species vary in their ability to meter their caloric intake as the caloric content of their diet changes. Rats are very accurate caloric regulators, dogs are relatively poor at it, and man lies somewhere in between. For example, rats consume about 22 grams of food daily when the caloric density of the food is 4.0 Kcal. per gram. Caloric dilution to 2.4 Kcal./gram, by the addition of non-nutritive cellulose, results in an increase in food intake of about 50 percent. Caloric concentration to 5.1 Kcal./gram, by the addition of corn oil, results in a 20 percent decrease in food consumption.[55] Furthermore, the rat can regulate energy balance without the participation of the oropharyngeal receptors. Rats trained to derive all of their nutriments from food self-injected directly into the stomach are perfectly capable of caloric regulation.

Dogs, however, do not compensate rapidly for a caloric alteration of the diet.[55, 57] They need several days or even weeks to modify eating habits and regulate energy input. After a 25 percent caloric dilution, they compensate only moderately by the end of a 10-day period. Gastric preloads of less than one-third of normal intake are also ineffective in reducing subsequent food intake.[58] But, with enough time, dogs can learn to regulate energy balance if given stomach loads greater than 30 percent of their normal intake.[60] Following a 50 percent preload, they decrease food intake by about 50 percent. Following a 100 percent preload, food intake may decrease as much as 95 percent. A load of 175 percent, however, is necessary to reduce intake levels to near zero.

The effects of the volume and the caloric content of gastric loads interact in the production of satiety.[11] When rats are deprived of food for 15 hours and given an intragastric load of either 6 or 12 milliliters of isotonic saline or a highly nutritive liquid diet, eating decreases as load volume increases. When load volume is held constant, meal size decreases as caloric content increases. Regardless of the volume of the loads, food consumption is smaller after a nutritive than after a non-nutritive load. Loads also affect the interval of time between the loading and the first meal: the greater the load or the greater the caloric content of the load, the greater the intermeal interval. It thus appears that satiety signals not only originate from the stomach, as in the case of the 6-milliliter loads, but also from the intestine, as in the case of the 12-milliliter loads. Furthermore, these signals seem to summate in their inhibitory effects upon eating behavior.

ENTEROGASTRONE. Gastric motility decreases or even stops following the partial emptying of the contents of the stomach into the duodenum. This phenomenon results from a hormonal feedback system between the duodenum and the stomach. The presence in the duodenum of fats or carbohydrates, along with a high degree of acidity, results in the secretion of enterogastrone from the duodenal walls. This hormone, which travels through the blood stream, produces inhibition of gastric motor activity.[42, 101] Although early attempts to induce satiety with enterogastrone failed,[56] more recently, injections of enterogastrone have been shown to induce anorexia.[107]

OSMOTIC EFFECTS. Satiety can result from an increase in osmotic pressure in the gastrointestinal lumen. Intragastric loads of hypertonic saline solutions can induce satiety.[115] If water-deprived rats are intragastrically loaded with 3 milliliters of either hypertonic glucose (20 or 40 percent) or saline (4 or 8 percent), they stop eating solid food and begin drinking of a 5.3 percent glucose solution.[74] However, other investigators, also testing water-deprived animals, found that although hypertonic saline does increase water intake, glucose loads actually decrease it.[53] The latter findings have been confirmed in animals that have not been water-deprived.[10] It is apparent that many foodstuffs, such as glucose, have a dual inhibitory action, one by way of their osmotic properties and the other by way of their metabolic effects.

SENSORY MECHANISMS. The location of hunger and satiety feelings in the gastrointestinal tract could not occur without involving the sensory nerves of the gut.[43] Although very few details are known about this sensory system, nerve endings of the sensory type have been found throughout the various layers of the stomach and intestine walls. Both the vagus and the splanchnic nerves carry motor and sensory fibers to and from the stomach. It has been estimated that about 80 percent of the vagal fibers and 50 percent of the splanchnic fibers carry sensory information.[2, 39]

Distention of the stomach with either a balloon or food results in an increase in the tension of the gastric wall as well as an increase in the pressure within the stomach and intestines. These changes excite tension and pressure receptors located in the outer layers of the gastrointestinal wall. A linear relationship appears to exist between the frequency of discharge of these receptors and the degree of distention. The nerve impulses from the stomach are then transmitted, by way of the vagal and splanchnic systems, to the brain.[8, 51, 89]

The increased firing rate of the vagus nerve observed after injection of hypertonic solutions into the stomach and the intestine suggests the existence of an osmoreceptor system, sensitive to the concentration of the stomach contents.[90, 117] Stomach emptying rate is known to decrease after a hypertonic load has been introduced into the stomach or the duodenum.[50, 112] The fact that local anesthetization of the gastrointestinal mucosa does not reduce the inhibitory action of hypertonic solutions in the stomach suggests that the osmoreceptors may be located deep in the gut wall, and that the solutions must be absorbed into the wall before the osmoreceptors can be excited.[112]

Little is known of the role gastric and duodenal acidity play in feeding, although gastric motility is inhibited by the infusion of acid solutions into the duodenum.[96] This effect must be mediated by the nervous system, since the motility of a Heidenhain pouch is inhibited only if the pouch's nerves remain intact.[123] It is not known whether the effects of acidity on motility also influence hunger or satiety.

The gastrointestinal tract may also have receptors specifically sensitive to glucose and certain amino acids,[86, 110, 113] since an increase in the firing rate of the stomach nerves of cats, dogs, and man follows the introduction of glucose or amino acids into the stomach. There even seems to be a primitive neural coding, since some fibers respond only to glucose, while others respond only to amino acids.

There is no doubt that the gastrointestinal system plays an important role in satiety mechanisms. The mechanical, physico-chemical, and biochemical actions of food in the gut activate both hormonal and neural mechanisms. They act not only on the intestinal tract itself but also on the brain, thus providing feedback systems that help regulate the intake of food.

BIBLIOGRAPHY

1. Adrian, E. D. The electrical activity of the mammalian olfactory bulb. *EEG. Clin. Neurophysiol.* 2 (1950): 377–388.
2. Agostoni, E.; Chinnock, J. E.; Daly, M. De B.; and Murray, J. G. Functional and histological studies of the vagus nerve and its branches to the heart, lungs and abdominal viscera in the cat. *J. Physiol. (London)* 135 (1957): 182–205.
3. Allen, W. F. Distribution of cortical potentials resulting from insufflation of vapors into the nostrils and from stimulation of the olfactory bulbs and the pyriform lobe. *Amer. J. Physiol.* 139 (1943): 553–555.
4. ———. Effect of ablating the pyriform-amygdaloid areas and hippocampi on positive and negative olfactory conditioned reflexes and on conditioned olfactory differentiation. *Amer. J. Physiol.* 132 (1941): 81–92.
5. ———. Effects of prefrontal brain lesions on correct conditioned differential responses in dogs. *Amer. J. Physiol.* 139 (1943): 525–532.
6. Allison, A. C. The morphology of the olfactory system in the vertebrates. *Biol. Rev.* 28 (1953): 195–244.
7. Amoore, J. E. Current status of the steric theory of odor. *Ann. N. Y. Acad. Sci.* 116 (1964): 457–476.

8. Anand, B. K., and Pillai, R. V. Activity of single neurons in the hypothalamic feeding centres: effect of gastric distension. *J. Physiol. (London)* 192 (1967): 63–77.

9. Bacon, W. E.; Snyder, H. L.; and Hulse, S. H. Saccharin preference in satiated and deprived rats. *J. Comp. Physiol. Psychol.* 55 (1952): 112–114.

10. Balagura, S. Influence of osmotic and caloric loads upon lateral hypothalamic self-stimulation. *J. Comp Physiol. Psychol.* 66 (1968): 325–328.

11. ———, and Coscina, D. V. Influence of gastrointestinal loads on meal-eating patterns. *J. Comp. Physiol. Psychol.* 69 (1969): 101–106.

12. Balagura, S., and Fibiger, H. C. Tube Feeding: intestinal factors in stomach loading. *Psychon. Sci.* 10 (1968): 373–374.

13. Beattie, J., and Sheehan, D. The effects of hypothalamic stimulation on gastric motility. *J. Physiol. (London)* 81 (1934): 218–277.

14. Bekesy, G. von. *Sensory inhibition.* Princeton: Princeton Univ. Press, 1967.

15. ———. Sweetness produced electrically on the tongue and its relation to taste theories. *J. Appl. Physiol.* 19 (1964): 1105–1113.

16. ———. Taste theories and the chemical stimulation of single papillae. *J. Appl. Physiol.* 21 (1966): 1–9.

17. Benjamin, R. M. Some thalamic and cortical mechanisms of taste. In *Olfaction and taste,* ed. Y. Zotterman, pp. 309–329. New York: Pergamon Press, 1963.

18. ———, and Akert, K. Cortical and thalamic areas involved in taste discrimination in the albino rat. *J. Comp. Neurol.* 111 (1959): 231–260.

19. Bennet, Marvin H. The role of the anterior limb of the anterior commissure in olfaction. *Physiol. Behav.* 3 (1968): 507–515.

20. Berkun, M. M.; Kessen, M. L.; and Miller, N. E. Hunger-reducing effects of food by stomach fistula versus food by mouth measured by a consummatory response. *J. Comp. Physiol. Psychol.* 45 (1952): 550–554.

21. Bernard, C. Leçons de physiologie experimentale appliquee a la medicine. *Cours du semestre d'ete,* 1855. vol. II, pp. 49–52. Paris: Bailliere, 1856.

22. Berry, C.; Hagamen, W.; and Hinsey, J. Distribution of potentials following stimulation of olfactory bulbs in the cat. *J. Neurophysiol.* 15 (1952): 139–148.

23. Blomquist, A. J., and Antern, A. Gustatory deficits produced by medullary lesions in the white rat. *J. Comp. Physiol. Psychol.* 63 (1967): 439–443.

24. Bodian, D. The non-olfactory character of the hippocampus as shown by experiments with poliomyelitis virus. *Anat. Rec.* 106 (1950): 178.

25. Borer, K. T. Disappearance of preferences and aversions for sapid solutions in rats ingesting untasted fluids. *J. Comp. Physiol. Psychol.* 65 (1968): 213–221.

26. ———, and Epstein, A. N. Disappearance of salt and sweet preferences in rats drinking without taste and smell. *Physiologist* 8 (1965): 118.

27. Brown, T.; Rosvald, H.; and Mishkin, M. Olfactory discrimination after temporal lobe lesions in monkeys. *J. Comp. Physiol. Psychol.* 56 (1963): 190–195.

28. Callens, M. *Peripheral and central regulatory mechanisms of the excitability in the olfactory system.* Brussels: Presses Academiques Europeennes S.C., 1967.

29. Cannon, W. B., and Washburn, A. L. An explanation of hunger. *Amer. J. Physiol.* 29 (1912): 444–454.

30. Carlson, A. J. The hunger contractions of the empty stomach during prolonged starvation. *Amer J. Physiol.* 33 (1914): 95–118.

31. Clark, W. E. Le Gros. Inquiries into the anatomical basis of olfactory discrimination. *Proc. Roy. Soc. (London), B,* 146 (1957): 299–319.

32. ———. The projection of the olfactory epithelium on the olfactory bulb of the rabbit. *J. Neurol. Neurosurg. Psychiat.* 14 (1951): 1–10.

33. ———, and Meyer, M. The terminal connections of the olfactory tract in the rabbit. *Brain* 70 (1947): 304–328.

34. Cohn, G. *Die organischen Geschmackstaffe.* Berlin: Siemenroth, 1914.

35. Crosby, E. C.; Humphrey, T.; and Lauer, W. E. *Correlative anatomy of the nervous system.* New York: Macmillan, 1962.

36. Davenport, H. *Physiology of the digestive tract.* Chicago: Year Book, 1966.

37. Erickson, R. P. Sensory neural patterns and gustation. In *Olfaction and taste,* ed. Y. Zotterman, pp. 205–213. New York: Pergamon Press, 1963.

38. Evans, D. R. Chemical structure and stimulation by carbohydrates. In *Olfaction and taste,* ed. Y. Zotterman, pp. 165–176. New York: Pergamon Press, 1963.

39. Foley, J. O. The functional types of nerve fibers and their numbers in the great splanchnic nerve. *Anat. Record* 100 (1948): 766–767.

40. Geldard, F. A. *The human senses.* New York: John Wiley & Sons, 1953.

41. Gesteland, R. C.; Lettvin, J. Y.; Pitts, W. H.; and Rojas, A. Odor specificities of the frog's olfactory receptors. In *Olfaction and taste,* ed. Y. Zotterman, pp. 19–34. New York: Pergamon Press, 1963.

42. Grossman, M. I. Gastrointestinal hormones. *Physiol. Rev.* 30 (1950): 33–90.

43. ———, and Stein, I. F. Vagotomy and hunger-producing action of insulin in man. *J. Appl. Physiol.* 1 (1948): 263–269.

44. Halpern, B. P. Chemical coding in taste-temporal patterns. In *Olfaction and taste,* ed. Y. Zotterman, pp. 275–284. New York: Pergamon Press, 1963.

45. Hamilton, C. L. Rat's preference for high fat diets. *J. Comp. Physiol. Psychol.* 58 (1964): 459–460.

46. Hausmann, M. F. The behavior of albino rats in choosing foods. II. Differentiation between sugar and saccharin. *J. Comp. Psychol.* 15 (1933): 419–428.

47. Heimburg, R. von, and Hollerbeck, G. Inhibition of gastric secretion in dogs by glucagon given intraportally. *Gastroenterology* 47 (1964): 531–535.

48. Helmholtz, H. L. F. von. Ueber die Theorie der zusammengesetzen Farben. *Ann. Phys. Chem.* 163 (1852): 45–66.

49. Hoelzel, F. Central factors in hunger. *Amer. J. Physiol.* 82 (1927): 665–671.

50. Hunt, J. N., and Pathak, J. D. The osmotic effects of some simple molecules and ions on gastric emptying. *J. Physiol.* (*London*) 154 (1960): 254–269.

51. Iggo, A. Tension receptors in the stomach and urinary bladder. *J. Physiol.* (*London*) 128 (1955): 593–607.

52. Inglefinger, F. J. The late effects of total and subtotal gastrectomy. *New Engl. J. Med.* 231 (1944): 321–327.

53. Jacobs, H. L. Evaluation of the osmotic effects of glucose loads in food satiation. *J. Comp. Physiol. Psychol.* 57 (1964): 309–310.

54. ———. Observations on the ontogeny of saccharine preference in the neonate rat. *Psychonom. Sci.* 1 (1964): 105–106.

55. ———, and Sharma, K. N. Taste versus calories: sensory and metabolic signals in the control of food intake. *Ann. N. Y. Acad. Sci.* 157 (1969): 1084–1125.

56. Janowitz, H. D., and Grossman, M. I. Effect of prefeeding alcohol and bitters on food intake of dogs. *Amer. J. Physiol.* 164 (1951): 182–186.

57. ———. Effect of variations in nutritive density on intake of food of dogs and rats. *Amer. J. Physiol.* 158 (1949): 184–193.

58. ———. Some factors affecting the food intake of normal dogs and dogs with esophagostomy and gastric fistula. *Amer. J. Physiol.* 159 (1949): 143–148.

59. ———; and Hanson, M. E. Effect of intravenously administered glucose on food intake in the dog. *Amer. J. Physiol.* 156 (1949): 87–91.

60. Janowitz, H. D., and Hollander, F. Effect of prolonged intragastric feeding on oral ingestion. *Fed. Proc.* 12 (1953): 72.

61. Kennedy, G. C. The hypothalamic control of food intake in rats. *Proc. Roy. Soc.* (*London*), *B,* 137 (1950): 535–548.

62. Kimura, K., and Beidler, L. M. Microelectrode study of taste receptors of rat and hamster. *J. Cell. Comp. Physiol.* 58 (1961): 131–140.

63. Kohn, M. Satiation of hunger from food injected directly into the stomach versus food ingested by mouth. *J. Comp. Physiol. Psychol.* 44 (1951): 412–422.

64. Kurotsy, T.; Takeda, M.; and Ban, T. Studies on the gastrointestinal motility and hemorrhage induced by hypothalamic stimulation of rabbits. *Med. J. Osaka Univ.* 2 (1951): 97–120.

65. LeMagnen, J. Effets des administrations post-prandiales de glucose sur l'établissement des appétits. *C. R. Soc. Biol. Paris* 153 (1959): 212–215.

66. ———. Effects d'une pluralité de stimuli alimentaires sur le déterminisme quantitatif de l'ingestion chez le rat blanc. *Arch. Sci. Physiol.* 14 (1960): 411–419.

67. ———. Le controle sensorial dans la régulation de l'apport alimentaire. *Probl. Actuel Endocrinol. Nutr.* 7 (1963): 147–171.

68. ———. Peripheral and systemic actions of food in the caloric regulation of intake. *Ann. N. Y. Acad. Sci.* 157 (1969): 1126–1156.

69. ———. Le processus de discrimination par le rat blanc des stimuli sucrés alimentaires et non alimentaires. *J. Physiol.* (*Paris*) 46 (1954): 414–418.

70. Lorber, S., and Shay, H. The effect of insulin and glucose on gastric motor activity of dogs. *Gastroenterology* 43 (1965): 564–574.

71. Luckhardt, A. B., and Carlson, A. J. Contributions to the physiology

of the stomach. XVII: On the chemical control of the gastric hunger mechanism. *Amer. J. Physiol.* 36 (1915): 37–46.

72. MacDonald, R.; Inglefinger, F. J.; and Belding, H. Late effects of total gastrectomy in man. *New Engl. J. Med.* 237 (1947): 887–896.

73. Masserman, J. H., and Haertig, E. W. The influence of hypothalamic stimulation on intestinal activity. *J. Neurophysiol.* 1 (1938): 350–356.

74. McCleary, R. A. Taste and postingestion factors in specific-hunger behavior, *J. Comp. Physiol. Psychol.* 46 (1953): 411–421.

75. Meyer, M., and Allison, A. An experimental investigation on the connections of the olfactory tracts in the monkey. *J. Neurol. Neurosurg. Psychiat.* 12 (1949): 274–286.

76. Miller, N. E., and Kessen, M. L. Reward effects of food via stomach fistula compared with those of food via mouth. *J. Comp. Physiol. Psychol.* 45 (1952): 555–564.

77. Moncrieff, R. W. *The chemical senses.* London: Leonard Hill, 1967.

78. ———. The odorants. Basic odor research correlation. *Ann. N. Y. Acad. Sci.* 58 (1954): 73–82.

79. Mook, D. G. Oral and postingestional determinants of the intake of various solutions in rats with esophageal fistulas. *J. Comp. Physiol. Psychol.* 56 (1963): 645–659.

80. ———, and Kozub, F. J. Control of sodium chloride intake in the nondeprived rat. *J. Comp. Physiol. Psychol.* 66 (1968): 105–109.

81. Morest, D. K. Projections of the nucleus of the tractus solitarius and area postrema in the cat. *J. Comp. Neurol.* 130 (1967): 277–293.

82. Moulton, D. G. Spatio-temporal patterning of response in the olfactory system. In *Olfaction and taste,* ed. T. Hayashi, pp. 109–116. Oxford: Pergamon Press, 1965.

83. Mozell, M. M., and Pfaffman, C. The afferent neural processes in odor perception. *Ann. N. Y. Acad. Sci.* 58 (1954): 98–108.

84. Müller, Johannes. *Handbuch der Physiologie des Menschen.* Coblenz: Hölscher, 1844.

85. Nachman, M. Learned aversion to the taste of lithium chloride and generalization to other salts. *J. Comp. Physiol. Psychol.* 56 (1963): 343–349.

86. Niijima, A. Afferent impulse discharges from glucoreceptors in the liver of the guinea pig. *Ann. N. Y. Acad. Sci.* 157 (1969): 690–700.

87. Oakley, B., and Pfaffman, C. Electrophysiologically monitored lesions in the gustatory thalamic relay of the albino rat. *J. Comp. Physiol. Psychol.* 55 (1962): 155–160.

88. Oertly, E., and Myers, R. G. A new theory relating constitution to taste. *J. Amer. Chem. Soc.* 41 (1919): 855–867.

89. Paintal, A. S. A study of gastric stretch receptors: Their role in the peripheral mechanism of satiation of hunger and thirst. *J. Physiol. (London)* 126 (1954): 255–270.

90. ———. Responses from mucosal mechanoreceptors in the small intestine of the cat. *J. Physiol. (London)* 139 (1957): 353–368.

91. Pfaffman, C. Gustatory afferent impulses. *J. Cell. Comp. Physiol.* 17: (1951): 243–258.

92. ———. Gustatory nerve impulses in rat, cat and rabbit. *J. Neurophysiol.* 18 (1954): 429–440.

93. ———. The sense of taste. In *Handbook of physiology.* Vol. 1,

Neurophysiology, pp. 507–533. Washington, D. C.: Amer. Physiol. Soc., 1959.

94. ———. Taste, its sensory and motivating properties. *Amer. Sci.* 52 (1964): 187–206.

95. ———. Taste preference and aversion following lingual denervation. *J. Comp. Physiol. Psychol.* 45 (1952): 393.

96. Pincus, I. J.; Friedman, N. H. F.; Thomas, J. E.; and Rehfuss, M. E. A quantitative study of the inhibitory effect of acid in the intestine on gastric secretion. *Amer. J. Digest. Diseases* 11 (1944): 205–208.

97. Quigley, J. P. The role of the digestive tract in regulating the ingestion of food. *Ann. N. Y. Acad. Sci.* 63 (1955): 6–14.

98. ———, and Hallaran, W. R. The independence of spontaneous gastrointestinal motility and blood-sugar levels. *Amer. J. Physiol.* 100 (1932): 102–110.

99. Quigley, J. P.; Johnson, V.; and Solomon, E. I. Action of insulin on the motility of the gastrointestinal tract. I: Action on the stomach of normal fasting man. *Amer. J. Physiol.* 90 (1929): 89–98.

100. Quigley, J. P., and Templeton, R. Action of insulin on the motility of the gastrointestinal tract. IV. Action on the stomach following double vagotomy. *Amer. J. Physiol.* 91 (1930): 482–487.

101. Quigley, J. P.; Zettelman, H. J.; and Ivy, A. C. Analysis of the factors involved in gastric inhibition by fats. *Amer. J. Physiol.* 108 (1934): 643–650.

102. Ramon y Cajal, S. *Histologie du systeme nerveux de l'homme et des vertebres.* Paris: Maline, 1911.

103. Richter, C. P. Transmission of taste sensation in animals. *Trans. Amer. Neurol. Assoc.* 65 (1939): 49–50.

104. Robins, R. B., and Boyd, T. E. The fundamental rhythm of the Heidenhain pouch movements and their reflex modifications. *Amer. J. Physiol.* 67 (1923): 166–172.

105. Rose, J., and Woolsey, C. Potential changes in the olfactory brain produced by electrical stimulation of the olfactory bulb. *Fed. Proc.* 2 (1943): 42.

106. Rzoska, J. Bait shyness, a study in rat behavior. *Brit. J. animal Behav.* 1 (1953): 128–135.

107. Schally, A. V.; Redding, T. W.; Lucien, H. W.; and Meyer, J. Enterogastrone inhibits eating by fasted mice. *Science* 157 (1967): 210–211.

108. Scott, W. W.; Scott, C. C.; and Luckhardt, A. B. Observations on the blood sugar level before, during and after hunger periods in humans. *Amer. J. Physiol.* 123 (1938): 243–247.

109. Share, I.; Martyniuk, E.; and Grossman, M. I. Effect of prolonged intragastric feeding on oral food intake in dogs. *Amer. J. Physiol.* 169 (1952): 229–235.

110. Sharma, K. N., and Nasset, E. S. Electrical activity in mesenteric nerves after perfusion of gut lumen. *Amer. J. Physiol.* 202 (1962): 725–730.

111. Sheffield, F. D., and Roby, T. Reward value of a non-nutritive sweet taste. *J. Comp. Physiol. Psychol.* 43 (1950): 471–481.

112. Sircus, W. Studies on the mechanisms in the duodenum inhibiting gastric secretion. *Quart. J. Exptl. Physiol.* 43 (1958): 114–133.

113. Sirotin, B. Z. Electrophysiological study of reception from certain

internal organs in man. Report I: Impulses from receptors of the resected stomach and small intestine. *Bull. Exp. Biol. Med. U.S.S.R.* (English trans.) 50 (1961): 873–877.

114. Smith, D. F., and Balagura, S. Role of oropharyngeal factors in LiCl Aversion. *J. Comp. Physiol. Psychol.* 69 (1969): 308–310.

115. Smith, M., and Duffy, M. Some physiological factors that regulate eating behavior. *J. Comp. Physiol. Psychol.* 50 (1957): 601–608.

116. Stunkard, A., and Plescia, A. D. The effect of IV administration of various nutrients on the hunger gastric contractions of a man with severe brain damage. *Amer. J. Clin. Nutrition* 5 (1957): 203–211.

117. Sudakov, K. V., and Rogacheva, S. K. The afferent and efferent activity of the gastric fibers of the vagus nerve during tasting and after taking food. *Fed. Proc.* (trans. suppl.) 22 (1963): 306–310.

118. Sudsaneh, S., and Mayer, J. Relation of metabolic events to gastric contractions in the rat. *Amer. J. Physiol.* 197 (1959): 269–273.

119. Swann, H. The function of the brain in olfaction. *J. Comp. Neurol.* 50 (1934): 175–202.

120. ———. The function of the brain in olfaction. *Amer. J. Physiol.* 111 (1935): 257–262.

121. Templeton, R. D., and Quigley, J. P. Action of insulin on motility of gastrointestinal tract. II. Action on Heidenhain pouch. *Amer. J. Physiol.* 91 (1930): 467–474.

122. Tsang, Y. Hunger motivation in gastrectomized rats. *J. Comp. Psychol.* 26 (1938): 1–17.

123. Woodward, E. R.; Lyon, E. S.; Landor, J.; and Dragstedt, L. R. The physiology of the gastric antrum. Experimental studies on isolated antrum pouches in dogs. *Gastroenterology,* 27 (1954): 766–785.

SUGGESTED SUPPLEMENTARY READINGS

Grossman, M. I. Satiety signals. *Amer. J. Clin. Nutr.* 8 (1960): 562–567.
Sharma, K. N. Receptor mechanisms in the alimentary tract: their excitation and functions. In *Handbook of physiology,* sec. 6, vol. 1: *Alimentary canal,* pp. 225–237. Washington: Amer. Physiol. Soc., 1967.

CHAPTER 7

Specific Hungers

The term "specific hunger" is often used to mean the tendency of an organism to ingest materials of which it has been depleted and which are necessary for survival. However, this definition excludes cravings that do not correspond with any nutritional deficiency. Because the animal's tendency to ingest a specific foodstuff may have value in understanding eating behavior, a more useful definition of specific hunger is the tendency of an animal to ingest a certain foodstuff when given a choice, whether or not it coincides with any known nutritional deficiency. The opposite is also true: Animals can have aversions to a specific food, either because of past, aversive experience with it, or because their physiological condition dictates the aversion.

Specific Hungers in Humans

Children occasionally ingest chalk, dirt, ashes, or earth. The underlying cause for this behavior may be a deficiency of calcium, necessary for bone growth, or, in the case of materials with a powdery consistency, they may act as intestinal adsorbents, providing treatment for diarrhea. Certain types of earth are known to be rich in vitamin B, and their ingestion can cure a vitamin deficiency. Man, as do animals, can become coprophagic and eat feces, which contain large quantities of the microorganisms and enzymes necessary for production of the B-complex vitamins. Although these methods of replacing missing nutrients may be effective, the diseases brought about by such practices may be fatal. Ingestion of calcium in the form of wall paint, for example, may be followed by lead poisoning, while geophagia and coprophagia may result in severe infections.

In many cultural subgroups, it is the custom to go to a slaughterhouse and drink blood or eat raw liver. During the eighteenth and nineteenth centuries, when there was no satisfactory treatment for anemia, only the people who ate large quantities of liver or blood survived the disease.

An enhanced appetite for salt (sodium chloride) occurs in some patients suffering from a disease of the adrenal glands. Sodium is essential for life, and the hormone aldosterone, produced in the adrenal glands, prevents excessive loss of sodium through the urine. Patients with deficient adrenals do not produce enough aldosterone, and consequently lose large amounts of sodium. The increased ingestion of salt helps preserve their lives.

The hunger for certain foods does not always result from the "wisdom of the body." In many instances there are cultural or economic reasons for it. The proportions of carbohydrate, protein, and fat are approximately 55, 14, and 30, respectively, in the diet of people in wealthy cultures, and such a balance frequently leads to obesity. Carbohydrates constitute 90 percent of the diet in poor societies, providing bulk and calories and often resulting in malnutrition. Culture can alter the balance between the individual and his environment, and this can frequently lead to disease. The fact that some societies find polished rice more acceptable than unpolished rice, for example, can mean widespread beriberi, a deficiency in vitamin B.

Self-Selection of Diet

It is difficult to demonstrate the self-selection of foods by humans, since culture plays such a major role. Two typical and extreme examples are the great preference in the United States for milk and the great aversion to milk by the Chinese. It is easier to observe the self-selection of dietary components by animals in the wild, although their choices are often influenced by the availability of foodstuffs. This is particularly true among carnivores.

For a grazing ruminant living on a fertile terrain, food is available all year, or at least for long periods of time. Usually more than one type of grass or bush grows in the territory where the ruminant pastures. Most of the time a sheep, for example, will ingest more of a certain food, but one often observes a change in this pasturing animal's diet, and what previously constituted 10 percent of intake may become 80 percent. Moreover, in many cases a particular grass or leaf, constituting only a small percentage of the available vegetation, constitutes most of the diet. Sheep are thus continuously selecting only certain foodstuffs from a varied environment. Reports of occasional sarcophagia, osteophagia, and geophagia, when the food is poor in salts, make it clear that animals do select their diets, and that this selection is not the result of palatability alone, but also of bodily needs.

Selection of proper foodstuffs has to operate both quantitatively and qualitatively. In previous chapters we considered the quantitative regulation of feeding; now we will consider the qualitative regulation, based on the self-selection of adequate nutrients from a pool of possibilities, selection of a particular material as a response to a bodily depletion of that material, and aversion to particular foodstuffs.

No single foodstuff contains all of an animal's daily requirements for survival. Nevertheless, animals thrive in their natural habitats by selecting the various dietary components necessary for normal growth. This is especially true of omnivores, animals that eat both meat and plants.

To study self-selection in the laboratory, the animal is required to derive its entire food intake from various dishes containing different substances, as in a self-service cafeteria. The animal is offered pure chemical compounds, e.g.: casein for protein, sucrose or dextrose for carbohydrates, Crisco or olive oil for fats, solutions or powders of sodium chloride, potassium chloride, and calcium lactate for electrolytes, and solutions or mixtures of pure vitamins. This is seldom the case in nature, since a particular foodstuff contains various nutrients, and 2 or 3 different foods may provide the organism with all of its necessary requirements. Animals are, however, capable of selecting an adequate diet under laboratory conditions. For example, rats given a choice between a protein-free and a protein-rich diet chose the protein diet.[33] When given access to an assortment of nutritive substances in both solid and liquid form, including vitamin solutions, they select appropriate quantities of the various substances, grow normally, and maintain their normal motor and sexual activity.[44] They grow at the same rate as animals fed a standard laboratory diet, in spite of the fact that they actually ingest about 20 percent less food.

The dietary selections made by rats offered a variety of substances are not fixed, but actually respond to the animals' physiological needs. For example, as shown in Figure 7–1, female rats allowed to self-select their diet before, during, and after pregnancy modify their selection according to their changing condition.[40] As can be seen, carbohydrate intake was unaffected by pregnancy. Fat and protein intake increased moderately during pregnancy, and even more during the lactation period. When lactation was over, intake returned to normal. A similar pattern of behavior was observed with respect to the intake of sodium chloride, calcium lactate, and sodium phosphate solutions. The increases in protein, fat, and minerals reflect an increased need during pregnancy. While the mother rats on a self-selection diet ingested 20 percent less food than mothers on a stock diet, the weights of the mothers and their offspring were comparable. The self-selection rats apparently eat less because they can satisfy their increased appetite for minerals without ingesting a large amount of other, unneeded foodstuffs. On the stock diet, the rats that needed a high amount of calcium had to take a large amount of the entire diet.

The body is not infinitely wise, and under certain experi-

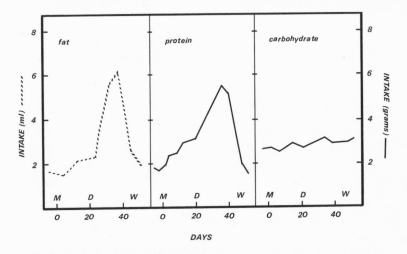

Figure 7–1. The preference of female rats for fats and proteins is enhanced during pregnancy and lactation. During these physiological states, carbohydrate selection is not affected. *M* = mating, *D* = delivery, *W* = weaning. Adapted from C. P. Richter and B. Barelare. *Endocrinology* 23 (1938): 15. Adapted with permission.

mental conditions, animals deriving their nutriments in the self-selection manner show inappropriate growth curves.[20, 35] Factors such as time spent on a certain diet, ratio between solid and liquid substances of the diet, number of rats in a cage, and sex of the animal all influence the dietary components selected. Experience with the selection of specific components, as well as the time permitted an animal to familiarize itself with the various substances, also have been shown to be critical.[17, 59] Ingestion of certain materials increases when they are soaked in water; this phenomenon is probably related to the finickiness observed in many animals about dry, powdered food. There is no good explanation for the finding that animals housed in groups in self-selection experiments are superior to animals housed individually, in terms of growth and body weight.[22] Sex appears to play an important role, in that females select better than males.[22, 40] This finding should be taken with caution, since the 2 sexes have different rates of growth, and this fact, rather than hormonal factors, may be responsible for the apparent superiority of females.

Food Selection As a Response to Specific Needs

The protein and amino acid contents of a diet may vary not only in terms of absolute quantities but also in terms of relative amounts of the various amino acids. It is possible to induce a protein deficiency with a diet that is normal in total quantity of protein but deficient in certain indispensable amino acids, i.e., those amino acids that cannot be synthesized from other amino acids by the organism. Proteins can be metabolized only if the amino acids that constitute them exist in a specific proportion. A deficiency of 1 of the component amino acids, even though there may be an excess of another, results, for all practical purposes, in a protein-deficient diet.

If a diet prepared of mixed amino acids is deficient in even 1 of them, there is a decrease in food consumption within 24 hours. Food consumption will normalize, however, if the diet is supplemented with the deficient amino acid, either by mixing it into the stock diet or injecting it directly into the animal.[11] A similar reduction in food intake can be produced by adding an excess of amino acids to a low protein diet, thus causing an amino acid imbalance. If a 6 percent casein, low protein diet is supplemented with a mixture of all the indispensable amino acids but histidine, animals will also reduce food intake.[15] Although the total number of amino acids is in fact increased, the low concentration of histidine becomes the limiting amino acid; adding histidine again results in increased food consumption and body weight.[16]

The concentration of amino acids in the blood reflects the amount and pattern of amino acid consumption. Amino acids in low concentrations in the diet are present in low concentrations in the blood; amino acids abundant in the diet are present in high concentrations in the blood. Some scientists have suggested that food consumption is dependent in part on blood amino acids.[1] However, it is not the total amount of amino acids that is being monitored by the body, but the amino acid patterns.[27,28] The suggestion is that an imbalanced diet causes an imbalance of amino acids in the blood; this is somehow sensed by the organism, and results in a decrease in food intake.

If a vitamin B-complex deficiency is created in rats by giving them a self-selection diet lacking baker's yeast, the feeding preference of the animals changes drastically.[46] As can be seen from the results depicted in Figure 7–2, carbohydrate and protein intake decrease, while at the same time fat intake increases. When B-complex vitamins were included in the diet, the animals ate great amounts of the yeast and recovered from the hypovitaminosis. Carbohydrate intake increased and fat intake decreased. The protein content of the baker's yeast rendered the protein derived from casein unnecessary. Only when consumption of the yeast decreased did casein intake reappear. It is now known that 2 of the B-complex vitamins (thiamine hydrochloride and riboflavin) are important coenzymes, necessary for the normal metabolism of carbohydrates and proteins. In their absence, ingestion of sucrose or casein would be superfluous, and perhaps even toxic, so, in order to fulfill its energy requirements, the animal increases fat intake. This is a dramatic illustration of a change in diet occurring when the organism is depleted of an important nutritional component.

Carbohydrate selection can be influenced by other means as well. As we have seen, food intake increases following administration of insulin, a pancreatic hormone that produces low blood sugar and increases glucose utilization.[3,23] If animals are given a choice between a glucose solution and their regular standard diet, insulin increases glucose intake without affecting normal diet intake.[37,53] Since insulin basically produces a need for glucose, the animals are responding appropriately. Intake of other digestible carbohydrates also increases. These results suggest the presence of a specific need for glucose or other utilizable carbohydrates, and

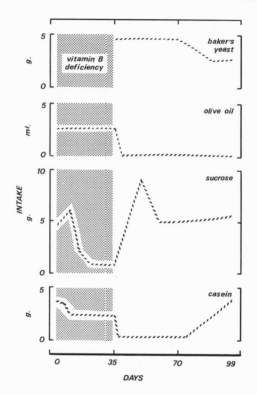

Figure 7–2. During a vitamin B-complex deficiency (shadowed area), rats decrease their carbohydrate (sucrose) and protein (casein) intake, and increase fat (olive oil) consumption. When the animals are given access to vitamins of the B-complex (baker's yeast), they change their preference back to carbohydrates and eventually proteins. Adapted from C. P. Richter, L. E. Holt, B. Barelare, and C. D. Hawkes, *Amer. J. Physiol.* 124 (1938): 596. Adapted with permission.

offer a contrast to the results obtained when sweet but non-nutritional saccharin rather than glucose is offered.

Rats prefer saccharin at a concentration of about 0.5 to 1.0 percent when other food is freely available. Food deprivation shifts the preference peak up to 3 percent.[2] Since saccharin is a sweet-tasting chemical which contains no calories, the deprived animals' need for calories is being reflected in an increased taste preference for sweets. However, these results were obtained in short-term tests, and the animals were not given the opportunity to experience the nutritionally useless effects of drinking saccharin. When given this opportunity, they learn not to be fooled by the sweet taste of saccharin.[52]

The same learning is evident when animals are injected with insulin and then given a 2-bottle test, 1 bottle containing glucose and the other fructose.[18] Glucose is less sweet than fructose, but it provides faster relief from the low blood sugar produced by insulin. The animals were given 2 tests with the 2 solutions. At first they preferred the sweeter fructose solution, but 24 hours later they had learned to prefer the glucose solution. It again seems apparent, as in the response to saccharin, that the need for carbohydrates is translated into the behavioral repertoire of hungry animals as a preference for sweets. Whether this taste preference is learned is not known, but when an animal is given a choice, it will go for the sweeter of 2 solutions. However, if the sweeter solution, does not contain calories, the animal eventually selects a less sweet but more calorically rewarding substance. It appears that a caloric-glucose need finally leads to a specific search for glucose.

If an animal is deprived of its own endogenous insulin, carbohydrate consumption is again altered. An organism can be made deficient in insulin by having its pancreas surgically removed or biochemically destroyed. Surgical removal of the pancreas results in a deficiency of insulin, glucagon, and pancreatic enzymes necessary for digestive processes. Under these conditions, animals decrease their consumption of carbohydrates.[43] However, the biochemical blockade with alloxan, which destroys only the insulin-secreting cells of the pancreas, provides a clearer technique for inducing insulin deficiency or diabetes, as it is known clinically. The glucose intake of animals in these circumstances increases and remains high until their death.[54]

Insulin, which increases carbohydrate consumption in normal animals, decreases it in diabetics. When diabetes is present, blood glucose levels increase from a normal level of 70 to 90 milligrams percent to up to 600 milligrams percent. However, the tissues remain relatively deficient in glucose, because glucose is easily metabolized by the tissues only if insulin is present. Thus, high levels of glucose circulate in the blood of the diabetic organism, but it is not well utilized, and there is still a need for it. Somehow the brain is able to detect this need and motivate the organism accordingly. Administration of insulin to a diabetic animal simply restores the tissue's utilization of glucose; the animal is no longer in need of glucose, and consequently decreases consumption of it.

An appetite for sodium salts occurs widely in nature [6] and has been intensively studied in the laboratory.[39] Although animals will ingest most of the common sodium salts, the one most preferred is sodium chloride (common table salt). A decrease in the circulating levels of sodium can lead to fatigue, nausea, anorexia, and eventual death. Animals submitted to a low sodium diet decrease food intake, become inactive, lose weight, and eventually die. When sodium in the blood is low, animals increase their intake of it and thus cure themselves. However, even perfectly healthy animals show an appetite for sodium.

Laboratory rats not deficient in sodium show a strong preference for mild solutions of sodium chloride. In a 2-bottle situation, with water in 1 bottle and varying concentrations of sodium chloride in the other, animals usually prefer the contents of 1 bottle over the other. If the concentration of the sodium chloride solution is below their threshold (approximately 0.001 molar), they will show no drinking preference. If the concentration of sodium is increased so that it can be tasted, the animals prefer to drink from the sodium rather than from the water bottle. The amount ingested is maximum at a 0.15 molar concentration. With concentrations of salt greater than 0.15 molar, the animals typically consume very little of the saline solution and switch to the water (see Figure 6–3).

If a state of sodium deficiency is created in animals, not only do they increase consumption of sodium salts, they even shift their peak preference to higher concentrations.[5, 7, 32, 34, 38] In man and other animals that sweat, an increased appetite for sodium follows strenuous exercise and profuse sweating,[24, 29] since sweat is rich in salt. Sodium intake also increases during pregnancy and lactation.[40] Rats increase their normal sodium intake up to 3 times during pregnancy; immediately after pregnancy is terminated, sodium intake decreases sharply. If the animals are then permitted to lactate, sodium intake increases again, to even greater levels than during pregnancy. When an organism sustains a sodium loss, for whatever reason, it responds with the behavioral compensation of increasing sodium intake.

Most sodium circulating in the blood is saved from being excreted in the urine by the action of the adrenal hormone aldosterone, which helps the kidneys retain it. In the absence of aldosterone, following removal of the adrenal glands, great quantities of sodium are lost in the urine. Richter and Eckert first showed in 1938 that adrenalectomized rats developed an increased appetite for sodium, even if the sodium was available only at a 3 percent concentration that is not normally preferred.[41] Only those animals that were permitted to drink the sodium solution survived. The appetite for sodium did not develop immediately following adrenalectomy, but appeared somewhat gradually. However, most animals showed a strong sodium appetite 3 days after surgery.

The gradual increment in sodium appetite has been explained as both a learning process and an innate mechanism. The animals may need to learn that drinking the sodium solution makes them feel better. On the other hand, animals that are not allowed to drink sodium until 5 to 10 days after adrenalectomy drink as much as experienced adrenalectomized animals. This suggests that the gradual onset of sodium appetite is due to a gradual onset of a sodium need.[8, 56] Once this appetite has been established, it can be reversed by injecting the animals with extracts of the adrenal gland or aldosterone.[12, 57]

Increased sodium appetite also occurs when sodium is artificially removed from the body by a process known as dialysis.[9, 10] Animals are injected in the abdominal cavity with an isotonic glucose solution, and a couple of hours are allowed for the sodium to diffuse; the sodium-rich fluid is then extracted from the abdominal cavity. This procedure permits the removal of 20 percent of the sodium in the body. Sodium depletion and an increased sodium appetite can also be produced by injecting toxic formalin under the skin.[55, 58] This disrupts the walls of the local blood vessels, and sodium in protein-rich plasma seeps into the damaged area. In this case, sodium is not lost from the organism; it is sequestered beneath the skin. This procedure produces a lowered blood sodium with a normal body sodium level. The results indicate that an increased appetite for sodium is related to alterations in the circulating sodium rather than to the absolute amount of sodium in the organism.

Specific hunger for thiamine, vitamin B_1, occupies an important position in the history of specific hungers. It was a common belief during the Middle Ages and even the beginning of modern times that animals eat what they eat in a fixed manner, predetermined and instinctive in character. The first experimental demonstration of the flexibility of animals in dietary matters did not occur until the first quarter of the twentieth century, when Harris and his co-workers made rats deficient in B-complex vitamins and showed that they were able to select from 2 diets the one containing vitamin B.[17] When the various vitamins of the B-complex were discovered and synthesized, it was possible to create a specific thiamine deficiency without influencing other components of the B-complex. This permitted more precise studies of the specific hunger for thiamine.

As we have seen, thiamine is an important compound in the metabolism of carbohydrates. Deficiency of thiamine occurs between 2 and 3 weeks after it has been deleted from the diet, or during increased need for vitamin B_1 because of fever, hyperactivity of the thyroid gland, or excessively high carbohydrate intake. During the early stages of this deficiency in humans, they complain of anorexia, muscle cramps, and muscle tenderness. Severe manifestations are increased anorexia, weight loss, paralysis, inflammation of the nerves, heart failure, and nonspecific changes in the electrical activity of the brain. The initial signs in rats are diminished food intake and weight loss; in latter stages there is also inflammation of nerves and motor impairment. The signs and symptoms can be rapidly reversed by administration of thiamine. Vitamin B_1 is normally found in meats and in whole-grain cereals.

While debated for some years, it now seems clear that the ability to seek and ingest needed thiamine is not innate, but must be learned. Rats made deficient in thiamine and offered a multiple choice of diets are incapable of making a correct choice. If, on the other hand, the thiamine-deficient rats are given only the diet containing thiamine for several days, and are then offered a multiple choice of diets, they select the thiamine-rich diet.[17] However, offering the choice of a thiamine-rich diet to a thiamine-deficient rat does not result in its selection unless it possesses taste properties that make it novel and appealing to the animal.[47,48] It thus appears that a learning mechanism normally operates in the adaptive selection of thiamine. Deficient animals are able to thrive even under the multiple choice situation if the solution of thiamine is very concentrated, and ingestion of a few drops is sufficient to provide relief of the feeling of sickness.[45] Under such circumstances, some animals are able to associate so rapidly ingestion of the thiamine solution with the relief it brings that the diet selection mistakenly appears unlearned.

Thiamine deficiency in animals also brings about an increase in the ingestion of feces.[42] Although a normal rat may ingest up to 30 percent of its feces, a thiamine-deficient rat will ingest all of its feces. Fecal matter is rich in thiamine as a result of the thiamine-producing bacteria normally existing in the intestine.

While thiamine selection is thought to be learned, it is not equally clear whether other specific hungers are learned or innate. It may be that for certain foods either learning or innate mechanisms are operative, depending on a given situation. Whatever the explanation, the fact remains that the whole animal kingdom has thrived for millions of years, using as its sole basis for food selection some sort of body wisdom.

The genetic or innate theory of specific hungers states that proper selection of a foodstuff results from the innate ability to make an association between a bodily need and the taste or odor of a particular substance. There is some support for this idea. Animals with apparently no previous experience with a bodily deficiency are able to make a proper food selection, even when seemingly too much time elapses between actual ingestion and beneficial aftereffects to permit normal learning mechanisms to operate.

It is also true that animals with experimentally induced bodily needs can, under some circumstances, ingest the proper substance without any delay and in the proper quantity to reduce their need. We have already seen that rats with a severe and prolonged need for sodium show an immediate and high initial intake of a 3 percent sodium chloride solution.[32] One study in particular appears to support the genetic theory.[21] Healthy, naive subjects, never before having experienced a sodium deficiency, were trained while thirsty to go to 1 side of a T-maze either for water or a sodium chloride solution. A sodium need was then created in half of the subjects by means of a subcutaneous injection of formalin; the other half received an innocuous injection of isotonic saline. The next day the animals were placed in a T-maze, but turning to the correct side was not rewarded. The rats originally trained with a sodium chloride solution and then depleted of sodium continued to run in the maze for a longer time than the other groups. This experiment provides a situation in which sodium need was absent during the training period and sodium reward was absent during the testing period. Under these conditions, the animals had no chance to associate sodium intake with sodium need, and thus no chance to learn that sodium would be beneficial. Nevertheless, they exhibited an increased hunger for sodium, as evidenced by their prolonged running to the place where sodium chloride had been available. Supporters of the genetic theory point out that optimal learning occurs when the delay between a response and a reward reinforcement is about one-half of a second.[19] Yet the delay between ingestion and the beneficial effects of ingested material is often several minutes or even hours. According to conventional learning theory, specific hungers could not possibly be the result of learning processes!

A learning theory of specific hungers predicts that proper selection of a foodstuff results from the learned association between ingestion of a given substance and its resulting corrective effects. In order to explain such learning in view of the delay noted above, some psychologists postulate that an animal makes a series of contiguous associations through time which help connect the initial ingestion with the subsequent postingestional effects. Others suggest that an aftertaste lingers for hours following a meal, and that an animal is able to associate the aftertaste with the resulting beneficial effects of the food ingested.

It is now known, in the case of a learned aversion to a particular food, that hours can indeed intervene between eating the food and the punishment that makes the animal avoid that food thereafter. It was first shown in the late 1950s that the adverse aftereffects from exposure to X-rays can be temporally separated from a particular meal by several hours and still produce a learned aversion to the food.[13] More recently, it was shown that the association between the taste of a particular fluid and the following irradiation sickness can occur even after delays of up to 12 hours,[26, 51] with the degree of aversion depending upon the amount of X-ray irradiation.[36]

Lithium salts, rather than X-rays, can also be used to produce temporary sickness.[4, 30] Lithium acts as a poison, and causes destruction of cells in such areas as the kidney, liver, and brain. Animals can survive lithium if it is given in moderate amounts, and will thereafter avoid the substances that were closely related to the taste of lithium, or to the lithium-induced sickness. In order for the association to occur, an animal must taste the solutions or foodstuffs.[50] For example, a saccharin solution will not be associated with sickness if it is given by way of a gastrointestinal load, thus by-passing the mouth. Under proper conditions, as with X-rays, animals learn to avoid a foodstuff even if there is a delay of several hours between ingestion of the test substance and administration of the lithium.[31]

The possibility of learning when there are long delays between ingestion and subsequent physiological effects is not limited to learned aversions.[14] When thiamine-deficient rats are given a saccharin solution to drink, and are then injected with thiamine either immediately or 30, 75, or 180 minutes later, most of the animals are able to associate the beneficial effects of thiamine with the saccharin solution. There is a limit to the delay interval, however, since thiamine injection 180 minutes after drinking the saccharin solution produces no learning.

There is no doubt that animals are capable of associating certain types of food with their positive or negative aftereffects, thus maximizing the possibility of their survival. It is still too early to accept either the genetic theory or the learning theory as the sole explanation of specific hungers. Both may be correct, depending on the nutritional state of the animal and the foodstuff involved. Finally, it may be that, although the actual mechanism of association involves learning, there is an innately provided predisposition or tuning of the organism which makes this type of learning possible and efficient.

BIBLIOGRAPHY

1. Almquist, H. J. Utilization of amino acids by chicks. *Arch. Biochem. Biophys.* 52 (1954): 197–202.
2. Bacon, W. E.; Snyder, H. L.; and Hulse, S. H. Saccharine preference in satiated and deprived rats. *J. Comp. Physiol. Psychol.* 55 (1952): 112–114.
3. Balagura, S. Conditioned glycemic responses in the control of food intake. *J. Comp. Physiol. Psychol.* 65 (1968): 30–32.
4. ———, and Smith, D. F. The role of lithium and environmental stimuli on the generalized learned aversion to NaCl in the rat. *Amer. J. Physiol.* 219 (1970): 1231–1235.
5. Bare, J. K. The specific hunger for NaCl in normal and adrenalectomized white rats. *J. Comp. Physiol. Psychol.* 42 (1949): 242–253.
6. Dalke, P. D.; Beeman, R. D.; Kandel, F. J.; Robel, R. J.; and Williams, T. R. Use of salt by elk in Idaho. *J. Wildlife Management* 29 (1965): 319–332.
7. Denton, D. A., and Sabine, J. R. The selective appetite for Na shown by Na deficient sheep. *J. Physiol. (London)* 157 (1961): 97–116.
8. Epstein, A. N., and Stellar, E. The control of salt preference in the adrenalectomized rat. *J. Comp. Physiol. Psychol.* 48 (1955): 167–172.
9. Falk, J. L. Serial sodium depletion and NaCl solution intake. *Physiol. and Behav.* 1 (1966): 75–77.

10. ———, and Lipton, J. M. Temporal factors in the genesis of sodium chloride appetite by intraperitoneal dialysis. *J. Comp. Physiol. Psychol.* 63 (1967): 247–251.

11. Frazier, L. E.; Wissler, R. W.; Stefler, C. H.; Woolridge, F. L.; and Cannon, P. R. Studies in amino acid utilization. I. The dietary utilization of mixtures of purified amino acids in protein-depleted adult albino rats. *J. Nutr.* 33 (1947): 65–83.

12. Fregly, M. J., and Waters, I. W. Effect of mineralocorticoids on spontaneous sodium chloride appetite of adrenalectomized rats. *Physiol. Behav.* 1 (1966): 65–74.

13. Garcia, J., and Kimeldorf, D. Temporal relationship within the conditioning of a saccharine aversion through radiation exposure. *J. Comp. Physiol. Psychol.* 50 (1957): 180–183.

14. Garcia, J.; Erving, C.; Yorke, C., and Koelling, R. Conditioning with delayed vitamin injections. *Science* 155 (1966): 716–718.

15. Harper, A. E., and Kumfa, U. S. Amino acid and protein requirement. *Fed. Proc.* 18 (1959): 1136–1142.

16. Harper, A. E.; Leung, P.; Yoshida, A.; and Rogers, Q. R. Some new thoughts on amino acid imbalance. *Fed. Proc.* 23 (1964): 1087–1092.

17. Harris, L. J.; Clay, J.; Hargreaves, F. J.; and Ward, A. Appetite and choice of diet. The ability of the vitamin B-deficient rat to discriminate between diets containing and lacking the vitamin. *Proc. Roy. Soc. (London), B* 113 (1933): 161–190.

18. Jacobs, H. L. Studies on sugar preference: I. The preference for glucose solutions and its modification by injections of insulin. *J. Comp. Physiol.* 51 (1958): 304–310.

19. Kimble, G. A. *Hilgard and Marquis' conditioning and learning.* New York: Appleton-Century-Crofts, 1961.

20. Kon, S. K. The self-selection of food constituents by the rat. *Biochem. J.* 25 (1931): 473–481.

21. Krieckhaus, E. E. "Innate recognition" aids rats in sodium regulation. *J. Comp. Physiol. Psychol.* 73 (1970): 117–122.

22. Lat, J. The relationship of individual differences in regulation of food intake, growth and excitability level of the central nervous system. *Physiol. Bohemoslov.* 5 (1956): 38–42.

23. Mackay, E. M.; Callaway, J. W.; and Barnes, R. H. Hyperalimentation in normal animals produced by protamine insulin. *J. Nutr.* 20 (1940): 59–60.

24. McCance, R. A. Experimental sodium chloride deficiency in man. *Proc. Roy. Soc. (London), B* 119 (1936): 245–268.

25. McDonald, D. G.; Stern, J. A.; and Hahn, W. W. Effects of differential housing and stress on diet selection, water intake, and body weight in the rat. *J. Appl. Physiol.* 18 (1963): 937–942.

26. McLaurin, W. Postradiation saccharine avoidance in rats as a function of the interval between ingestion and exposure. *J. Comp. Physiol. Psychol.* 57 (1964): 316–317.

27. Mellinkoff, S. M. Digestive system. *Ann. Rev. Physiol.* 19 (1957): 193–196.

28. ———; Frankland, M.; Boyle, D.; and Greipel, M. Relation between serum amino acid concentration and fluctuations in appetite. *J. Appl. Physiol.* 8 (1956): 535–538.

29. Moss, N. Some effects of high air temperatures and muscular exertion upon colliers. *Proc. Roy. Soc. (London)*, *B* 95 (1924): 181–200.

30. Nachman, M. Learned aversion to the taste of lithium chloride and generalization to other salts. *J. Comp. Physiol. Psychol.* 56 (1963): 343–349.

31. ———. Learned taste and temperature aversions due to lithium chloride sickness after temporal delays. *J. Comp. Physiol. Psychol.* 73 (1970): 22–30.

32. ———. Taste preferences for sodium salts by adrenalectomized rats. *J. Comp. Physiol. Psychol.* 22 (1962): 1124–1129.

33. Osborne, T. B., and Mendel, L. B. The choice between adequate and inadequate diets, as made by rats. *J. Biol. Chem.* 35 (1918): 19–27.

34. Pfaffman, C., and Bare, J. K. Gustatory nerve discharges in normal and adrenalectomized rats. *J. Comp. Physiol. Psychol.* 43 (1950): 320–324.

35. Pilgrim, F. J., and Patton, R. A. Patterns of self-selection of purified dietary components by the rat. *J. Comp. Physiol. Psychol.* 40 (1947): 343–348.

36. Revusky, S. Aversion to sucrose produced by contingent X-irradiations: temporal and dosage parameters. *J. Comp. Physiol. Psychol.* 65 (1968): 17–22.

37. Richter, C. P. Increased dextrose appetite of normal rats treated with insulin. *Amer. J. Physiol.* 135 (1942): 781–787.

38. ———. Salt taste thresholds of normal and adrenalectomized rats. *Endocrinology* 24 (1939): 367–371.

39. ———. Total self-regulatory functions in animals and human beings. *Harvey Lectures* 38 (1942–43): 63–103.

40. ———, and Barelare, B. Nutritional requirements of pregnant and lactating rats studied by the self-selection method. *Endocrinology* 23 (1938): 15–24.

41. Richter, C. P., and Eckert, J. F. Mineral metabolism of adrenalectomized rats studied by the appetite method. *Endocrinology* 22 (1938): 214–224.

42. Richter, C. P., and Rice, K. K. Self-selection studies on coprophagy as a source of vitamin B-complex. *Amer. J. Physiol.* 143 (1945): 344–354.

43. Richter, C. P., and Schmidt, E. C. H. Increased fat and decreased carbohydrate appetite of pancreatomized rats. *Endocrinology* 28 (1941): 179–192.

44. Richter, C. P.; Holt, L. E.; and Barelare, Nutritional requirements for normal growth and reproduction in rats studied by the self-selection method. *Amer. J. Physiol.* 122 (1938): 734–744.

45. ———. Vitamin B_1 craving in rats. *Science* 86 (1937): 354–355.

46. ———; and Hawkes, C. D. Changes in fat, carbohydrate and protein appetite in vitamin B deficiency. *Amer. J. Physiol.* 124 (1938): 396–402.

47. Rodgers, W. H. Specificity of specific hungers. *J. Comp. Physiol. Psychol.* 64 (1967): 49–58.

48. Rozin, P., and Rodgers, W. H. Novel diet preferences in vitamin deficient rats and rats recovered from vitamin deficiency. *J. Comp. Physiol. Psychol.* 63 (1967): 421–428.

49. Scott, E. M. Self-selection of diet. I. Selection of purified compounds. *J. Nutr.* 31 (1946): 397–406.

50. Smith, D. F., and Balagura, S. Role of oropharyngeal factors in LiCl aversion. *J. Comp. Physiol. Psychol.* 69 (1969): 308–310.

51. Smith, J. C., and Roll, D. L. Trace conditioning with X-rays as an aversive stimulus. *Psychon. Sci.* 9 (1967): 11–12.

52. Smith, M. P., and Capretta, P. J. Effective drive level and experience on the reward value of saccharin solutions. *J. Comp. Physiol. Psychol.* 49 (1956): 553–557.

53. Soulairac, A. Action de l'insuline sur la consommation de différents glucides chez la souris. *Compt. Rend. Soc. Biol.* 138 (1944): 119–120.

54. ———. L'appetit glucidique du rat au cours due diabete alloxamique. L'action de l'insuline et de l'extrait ante-hypophysaire. *Compt. Rend.* 226 (1948): 754–756.

55. Stricker, E. M., and Wolf, G. Blood volume and tonicity in relation to sodium appetite. *J. Comp. Physiol. Psychol.* 62 (1966): 275–279.

56. Weiner, I. H., and Stellar, E. Salt preference of the rat determined by a single-stimulus method. *J. Comp. Physiol. Psychol.* 44 (1951): 394–401.

57. Wolf, G. Effect of deoxycorticosterone on sodium appetite in intact and adrenalectomized rats. *Amer. J. Physiol.* 208 (1965): 1281–1285.

58. ———, and Steinbaum, E. A. Sodium appetite elicited by subcutaneous formalin: mechanisms of action. *J. Comp. Physiol. Psychol.* 59 (1965): 335–339.

59. Young, P. T. Food seeking drive: affective processes and learning. *Psychol. Rev.* 56 (1949): 98–121.

SUGGESTED SUPPLEMENTARY READINGS

Denton, D. A. Salt appetite. In *Handbook of physiology,* sect. 6, vol. 1: *Alimentary canal,* pp. 433–459. Washington: Amer. Physiol. Soc., 1967.

Harper, A. E.; Benevenga, N. J.; and Wohlhueter, R. M. Effects of ingestion of disproportionate amounts of amino acids, *Physiol. Rev.* 50 (1970): 428–558.

Lat, J. Self-selection of dietary components. In *Handbook of physiology,* sec. 6, vol. 1: *Alimentary canal,* pp. 367–386. Washington: Amer. Physiol. Soc., 1967.

Rozin, P., and Kalat, J. W. Specific hungers and poison avoidance as adaptive specializations of learning. *Psychol. Rev.* 78 (1971): 459–486.

Snapper, I. Food preferences in man: special cravings and aversions. *Ann. N. Y. Acad. Sci.* 63 (1955): 92–106.

CHAPTER 8

Malnutrition and Obesity

Malnutrition

Several hundred studies involving animals and dozens of studies of humans show that the presence of malnutrition caused by the low calorie, low protein, and low vitamin content of a diet can cause brain damage. Possibly never in man's history has a scientific finding had more serious social and biological implications. Nevertheless, while national governments are quick to ban a particular consumer product because of its potential dangers, we are still waiting to see malnutrition, a proven killer, officially banned from the dining tables of affluent societies.

The presence of decreased mental capacity in undernourished children has been recognized for many years. However, only since the recent discovery of the importance of protein synthesis in learning ability have nutritional deficits been seriously considered by scientists as an important determinant of brain function.

The typical case history of a malnourished child involves not only insufficient food but also various types of secondary infectious diseases and intestinal problems. The child is born to a poor and chronically undernourished mother whose family is already too large for her means. During the first few months of his life he is breast-fed. Around the third month of life he usually develops severe diarrhea and vomiting resulting from an excessively contaminated environment, often due to the lack of some basic hygienic habits. The baby loses weight and becomes extremely dehydrated. He cannot tolerate anything in his stomach, and soon depletes his minimal caloric and nutritive stores. His disease, in turn, increases the demand for nutrients in the body, and the result is even more severe malnutrition. By this time the baby is ready to be weaned and is given a series of watery solutions containing starch to control the diarrhea. Many infants die at this point. The survivors typically are kept on liquid and bland food diets which contain very little protein. From then on the under-privileged child is kept on a low protein and low calorie diet. He will not reach 1 year of age without contracting 1 or more of the chronic parasitic diseases of the intestines. The new intestinal dwellers obtain their basic proteins and calories from the child's own tissues; he is marked. A typical case, representative of millions around the world, is shown in Figure 8–1.

BRAIN GROWTH AND NUTRITION. Growth of the brain, as with any other tissue, results from the multiplication of cells during growth periods before and often soon after birth.[66] This growth of living tissue cannot occur if the necessary nutrient materials are not available. With the development of finer histological and biochemical techniques during the last 3 decades, it has been possible to detect and measure the various chemical components of the brain. Histological studies have shown that most of the brain's development prior to birth is due to an increase in the number of neurons and glial cells. Cellular proliferation continues during the postnatal period in several species, including man and rat.[62, 66] However, most of the brain's development during the postnatal period and early infancy is the result of increases in cell size.

It is possible to make such determinations because the nuclear DNA (deoxyribonucleic acid) content is constant for any given species,[7] e.g., 6.2 picograms per nucleus in rats, and 6.0 picograms per nucleus in humans. Thus, the total number of brain cells can be determined by dividing the total DNA of the brain by the nuclear DNA. When DNA content is constant, as at time of weaning for rats, it indicates that cellular proliferation in the

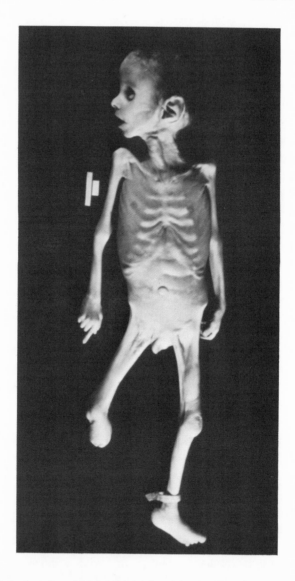

Figure 8–1. A malnourished child. Malnutrition lowered the child's capacity to defend itself against infections. During his short life span he was afflicted several times with intestinal, respiratory, and bone infections, the latter resulting in the amputation of his right leg. Courtesy and permission of Dr. Ira S. Schwartz, Mount Sinai Hospital Services, Elmhurst, N.Y.

brain has stopped.[21] If cell weight and cell protein remain constant, it indicates that cellular size is not changing.

During the postnatal period in rats, the brain does not develop homogeneously.[22] Cell proliferation stops first in the brainstem, later in the cerebellum, and finally in the neocortex. Although the cell proliferation period in humans extends several months postnatally, cell growth continues for several months more. Humans differ from rats in that a human's neocortex is the first structure in which cell proliferation stops; cells in other subcortical areas may proliferate for up to 12 months.[62]

Differences in brain growth at different stages of development suggest that interference with brain development at various times should produce different specific effects. For example, interfering with nutrition during the early postnatal period of cellular proliferation is more detrimental to an organism than interfering later, when only cellular size is changing. When newborn rats are fed well for the first 21 days of life, kept undernourished for the next 21 days, and then given unlimited food, they soon reach a growth–weight curve just under that of control animals. The same thing happens when rats are well nourished from birth to the ninth week, poorly nourished for 21 days, and then given free access to food.[59] However, rats that are poorly nourished during the *first* 21 days of life and then given free access to food grow slowly and develop into small-sized adults.[32, 60] While malnutrition at any time may reduce growth,[40] the growth reduction can be temporary if the period of undernutrition occurs after the early period of cell proliferation. However, if the malnutrition period coincides with this early proliferative period, the damage may be permanent.[64] In the latter case the animals also possess smaller heads and organs.

Comparable observations have been made in man. Severe early malnutrition in human infants leads to smaller body frames and lower body weights,[51] smaller brains,[10,67] lower intelligence quotients, and a decreased capacity to perform in various types of psychological tests.[13, 16, 19, 51] This is true of malnourished children all over the world, including the United States. The performance level of malnourished children can be improved by careful nutritional rehabilitation programs, but only when their malnutrition occurred after they were 1 or 2 years of age.[16, 19, 37] The retardation caused by malnutrition does not improve if the period of malnourishment occurred during the first months of life.[13, 15]

This is well illustrated by a 7-year study of some children in Gambia, a small country on the west coast of Africa.[51] Their growth was satisfactory during the first 4 to 6 months of life, and was similar to that of normal English children. Starting at the age of 6 months, their growth rate was stunted for about 8 months. Rate of growth then again became normal and remained so for the next 6 years. The loss from failure to gain weight during the period of stunted growth, however, was never recovered. Changes in growth rate during critical developmental periods can thus bring permanent deficiencies and, ultimately, leave a large residue of poorly functioning people who, in turn, rear their children under substandard conditions, eventually producing a new malnourished and deficient generation.[18] Sometimes such a tragic cycle is based on cultural styles of eating that transcend economic status.

Severe malnutrition in humans results in small head circumference, which is, in turn, an indirect measurement of brain size. It is now know that the 2 measures are correlated, especially during the first year of life. Children who die of malnutrition or one of its complications not only have smaller heads, but the circumference is linearly related to total brain DNA, and thus to the number of brain cells.[68] The number of brain cells is relatively reduced at least as much as the head circumference, and sometimes even more.

Proteins and amino acids are most necessary during the early development of the brain; the later increases in cell size are largely dependent on phospholipids, a complex fat compound abundant in neural tissue. When subjected to malnutrition, the organism makes several physiological changes in order to save protein, since with severe or prolonged malnutrition protein synthesis may be impaired. For example, severe malnutrition can result in specific enzymatic changes similar to those observed in a form of mental retardation known as *phenylketonuria.*[58] This is an innate metabolic disease in which lack of an enzyme makes it impossible for an amino acid, phenylalanine, to be converted to a second amino acid, tyrosine. The excess of phenylalanine depresses certain functions of the brain, and mental retardation results. Severely malnourished persons have an abnormally high level of phenylalanine.[17] This is a metabolic situation similar to that existing in mongolism, a most severe form of congenital mental retardation.[31]

The enzymes which help control chemical reactions in the brain are largely derived from vitamins which are usually deficient when malnutrition is present. These vitamins participate in all of the metabolic reactions that maintain the normal function of the nervous system. Prior to birth, the fetus is usually protected against severe avitaminosis if the mother receives adequate care, but vitamin deficiencies can occur in any other period of an individual's life. The earlier it occurs, the more detrimental its effects on the brain. The result of extreme cases of vitamin B deficiency, for example, may be death. A less severe deficiency produces irritability, lack of appetite, inflammation of both sensory and motor nerves, and even depression and mental dullness.[8] Lack of niacin, one of the enzyme members of the vitamin B-complex, may lead to severe mental collapse.[50] The absolute levels of niacin as well as the availability of two amino acids, tryptophane and leucine, are necessary for this enzyme to operate normally.[24] In other words, an imbalance between tryptophane and leucine can produce a depletion of niacin. Niacin deficiency, or pellagra, is not rare. Millions throughout the world depend on corn as the main staple of their diet, and corn is characteristically low in niacin.

For a long time it was thought that the fetus in the uterus was completely protected against any nutritional deficiencies. Because of the great extracting power of the placenta, even substances that were below normal in the mother's blood were thought to be available to the fetus in normal quantities. It is now known, however, that intrauterine malnutrition can occur, with extremely detrimental effects to the fetus.[63]

Severe malnutrition of a pregnant rat, either from restriction of calories or protein, results in a small placenta with fewer cells than normal. This is especially true if the malnutrition is imposed early in pregnancy. The offspring of such mothers are small and possess brains with 15 percent less than the normal number of neurons. Even if the newborns are adequately fed, they never recover and remain permanently deficient in brain cells. In addition, malnutrition during pregnancy greatly potentiates the deleterious effects of malnutrition in later life. If the offspring of malnourished mothers remain malnourished during their first 21 days of life, they show a 40 percent decrease in the number of brain cells!

Even though experiments in maternal malnutrition cannot be performed on humans, society unfortunately provides us with a number of human cases that replicate in almost every detail the laboratory work done with rats.[63] In one group of indigent pregnant women, 50 percent had poorly developed placentas! Even when malnourished mothers have normal placentas, as many as one-third of their babies can have congenital malformations. The DNA content of the brains of infants who die of malnutrition, after being born of malnourished mothers, can be as low as 40 percent of that seen in normal newborn infants. This is the same percentage that applied to the potentiating effect of malnutrition during pregnancy on the later effects of malnutrition in rats.

Some don't believe that malnourishment, by itself, can cause mental deficiency. They feel there has been a lack of consideration for cultural factors influencing psychological performance. According to them, the lower mental performance is not due to malnutrition but to the underprivileged cultural experiences of the people tested. Some experimenters have controlled for this factor, however, and still find mental deficits in malnourished groups. Even more important, cultural factors cannot affect the circumference of the head, the size or DNA content of the brain, or the number of brain cells. It seems most likely that the deficiencies in brain structure produced by malnutrition are translated into deficits in mental capacity.

The implications of this possibility for at least half of the population of the earth are staggering. Every human embryo, even with a normal genetic potential, may not have the opportunity to develop its full capacities. For many individuals, it is probably too late to reverse the mentally crippling effects of early malnutrition.

Anorexia Nervosa

Malnutrition is not always the result of a shortage of food. There is a form of pathological, self-imposed undernutrition that has been called *anorexia nervosa*.[5, 23, 48] This illness has been known for at least 100 years, but its treatment has not been improved. Anorexia nervosa afflicts more women than men, and it usually occurs in the young. There is a net reduction in caloric intake, which in severe cases may be reduced to zero, resulting in drastic malnutrition and death. More frequently, a persistent low caloric intake leads to a gradual reduction of body weight. The individual prefers a high protein, high fat, low carbohydrate diet, often of his or her own design.

Since the discovery of the important role the hypothalamus plays in regulation of feeding behavior, several attempts have been made to relate anorexia nervosa to disturbed hypothalamic function. These, as well as other attempts to find a primary physiological cause, have been fruitless. Although in women the disease is sometimes associated with hormonal disturbances, hormonal imbalances can usually be dissociated from the feeding disorder.

Anorexia nervosa is commonly accompanied by severe psychological disturbances involving affective and obsessive symptoms. There is often a pathological fear of becoming fat even though the individual is skeletal in appearance. Her concept of normal body weight is lowered, and she usually has a distorted perception of her body image.

Obesity

Although not as common as malnutrition, obesity—a disproportionate amount of fat usually resulting in overweight—has recently reached epidemic proportions in affluent countries where the individual's physical activity has decreased and his caloric intake increased.[61] Obesity can result from hereditary causes, acquired hormonal imbalances, physical disturbances of the nervous system, disturbed psychological states, or simply inactivity with too much food intake. A positive energy balance is a necessary condition for obesity to occur. Excess energy is stored as fat in specialized cells called adipose cells; this process is often facilitated by metabolic dysfunction. Obesity results when the organism miscalculates, and ingests nutriments in amounts greater than those necessary to maintain a state of equilibrium.

CONSEQUENCES OF OBESITY. The detrimental effects of obesity must be considered from at least two points of view: psychological and pathological. In our culture, obesity is considered an undesirable physical state. The obese individual is subjected to various sorts of social recrimination, in such forms as personal insult, the disillusion of a sexual relationship, or high insurance premiums. Obese individuals often create a world of rationalizations and fantasies in order to cope with their problems. The psychological consequences of obesity are varied.[4, 55] The obese person often distorts the mental picture of his own body.[56] During high school years he may be excluded from participating in certain games because of his body size. The period of heterosexual dating may bring with it severe, traumatic experiences. These stresses bring their toll to the interpersonal relations of the obese person as well as to his own private psychological world.

In general, obese persons have a shorter life span, and are often afflicted by liver disease, diabetes mellitus, and diseases of the blood vessels. Lifelong overnutrition shortens the life spans of rats as well, even though the diseases they manifest are the same as those of properly fed animals.[46, 47]

Obesity is usually associated with several metabolic changes, of which alteration of the tolerance for glucose is the best known.[30] Thirty minutes after a standard intragastric load of 100 grams of glucose is given into a normal, nonobese person, glycemia should be no higher than 180 milligrams percent, and should drop to normal levels in 2 hours. Obese persons often show higher glucose levels at 30 minutes and persistent hyperglycemia for the next 2 to 4 hours. Another easily tested metabolic reaction is the response to fasting. Fasting results in increased levels of ketones and free fatty acids in nonobese subjects, but these metabolic changes are often diminished in obese persons.[69]

The association of obesity and diabetes mellitus has been well documented.[70] Indeed, clinical manifestations of the disease often disappear following dieting. A typical case is that of a 45-year-old person, 30 percent overweight, who has recently become very thirsty and feels the need to eat frequently. Blood analysis reveals an abnormally elevated glucose. The suspicion of diabetes is confirmed with a glucose tolerance test. After reducing his weight by dieting, all clinical manifestations of diabetes may disappear; often the glucose tolerance test normalizes as well.[44] Conversely, diabetes mellitus can grow worse if the patient gains weight. Overeating produces further stress on an organism already deficient in insulin-dependent reactions. These observations have been experimentally confirmed. For example, with their pancreas partially removed, rats that do not show glucose in the urine (glycosuria), a condition most commonly associated with increased blood glucose and diabetes, become glycosuric when they are made obese.[9]

Obesity can also result in an excessive infiltration of fat into the liver. Mild fat infiltration may be innocuous, but severe infiltration impairs liver function and can result in cirrhosis of the liver—a progressive, degenerative disease that eventually causes circulatory problems and deficiencies in liver function.[52]

Obesity and cardiovascular disease have often been associated,[52] although it is not clear whether obesity is a contributory or causal entity in heart disease. It is known, however, that angina pectoris (heart pains) and sudden death from heart attack are more frequent in obese than in nonobese men.[29] Heart disease is often accompanied by high cholesterol, and the latter is usually found to be elevated in obese persons.[1, 33]

CAUSES OF OBESITY. Obesity can be acquired during the postnatal period, or it can be determined genetically.[38, 39] Extreme cases of genetically determined obesity are the so-called yellow obesity, the obese hyperglycemic syndrome observed in mice, and the Laurence–Moon–Biedl syndrome observed in man (characterized by mental retardation, extra digits, and obesity). However, obesity can be inherited by simple genetic determination of the number of fat cells an organism is to have. When both parents are obese, the child has an 80 percent chance of becoming obese; the probability decreases to 50 percent when only one parent is obese.[2]

Genetically determined increase in the number of adipose cells is probably one of the most frequent causes of obesity. Genetically obese people may even have a metabolic system that is quite distinct from that of other obese people. The genetically obese child, for example, can be born with a normal weight, with his later obesity resulting from a positive energy balance and an increased fat deposition in the already supernumerous adipose cells. It is not clearly understood whether fat deposition itself is abnormally facilitated in these people.

Obesity also can occur in subjects with a normal genetic background. In fact, it can be acquired at any period of life. Obesity may result from endocrine imbalance, as, for example, in Cushing's disease of the adrenal glands, which is characterized by increased activity of the adrenal cortex and overproduction of adrenal hormones. Diabetes mellitus, a disease in which the lack of insulin greatly decreases the efficiency of glucose utilization, also is often accompanied by increased food intake and obesity.

Certain brain lesions can result in extreme obesity.[3, 45] A typical case is that of a person who begins having headaches and changes in visual acuity, and then suddenly develops a voracious, uncontrollable appetite and gains weight, doubling body size in a few months. Medical tests, frequently verified by autopsy, often indicate the presence of a tumor in the hypothalamic region.

It is now known that acquired obesity may not be solely the result of an increase in the size of adipose cells, but may also result from the proliferation of adipocites.[21, 26, 27, 43, 65] In the latter case, a young animal or human that is overfed during its early life may increase the number of its fat cells, and in this respect become similar to a genetically obese subject. Overeating in a later period of development, without having been force-fed when young, results only in an increase of the size of fat cells. These distinctions may be important, especially for the treatment and prevention of obesity.

Overeating, other than the passive overeating to which an infant may be submitted, is not commonly associated with any primary physiological disturbance; it can be the result of cultural, learned influences. Some societies praise obesity, and overeating becomes a volitional act aimed at achieving a higher body weight and the accumulation of fat. In some lower-class groups obesity is actually a mark of affluence. Mothers will overfeed their children or themselves in order to look more prosperous and advance in the social strata.

Overeating may be a response to psychological states of depression or anxiety, during which a person may gain several pounds. It has been argued that these persons have not learned to discriminate hunger feelings from other internal psychological states. In fact, some obese people cannot feel the hunger pangs that, in lean subjects, are normally associated with gastric contractions.[36]

Overeating may also be a displacement activity or a defense mechanism. For example, a woman who is afraid of sexual relations may become superobese in order to decrease the probability of being courted. Severe neurosis can also be associated with overeating. A person may become an obsessive-compulsive eater; obesity resulting from a night eating compulsion is not uncommon.[54] In a typical case, the patient may suffer from insomnia and extremely voracious appetite during the night, and have no appetite at all during the day. Night eating is often directly related to psychological stress.

Overeating may also result from boredom. The only channel the person may have available for distraction is to prepare food and consume it in large quantities.

In the majority of cases, obesity is simply the result of overeating, although it may sometimes be caused by decreasing activity without decreasing energy input [11] (the net energy balance has to be positive before any fat is accumulated). As technological automation increases, activity requirements decrease. The energy expenditures that used to be required for walking or riding to work, washing clothes, or cooking have been minimized, while energy input has not been proportionally reduced. Consequently, obesity is becoming more and more prevalent.

EATING PARALLELS IN MAN AND RAT. Animal experimentation has served to enhance the understanding of the biological and psychological processes of human beings. In this respect the biopsychological study of food intake has been very rewarding. Recently, scientists have begun to coordinate their knowledge of feeding behavior and motivation obtained from animals and humans, and the 2 fields of study are highly complementary.[42, 49]

Animal experimentation has shown that destruction of the ventromedial hypothalamic area results in overeating, obesity, hypofunction of certain target organs (like the ovaries), and changes in reactivity and emotionality. Following a ventromedial hypothalamic lesion, animals become extremely vicious. Although such a rage syndrome has been associated mainly with lesions of the septal area,[34] it cannot be compared in intensity or duration with the rage produced by lesion of the ventromedial hypothalamus. Animals with ventromedial lesions typically attack the experimenter's glove, a pencil, or any object, placed in their cage. If a normal rat is introduced into a cage containing a ventromedially lesioned animal, the lesioned rat brutally attacks the visitor, disregarding its sex and size, and always drawing blood from it. The attacks are sudden and short and usually terminate with the intruder lying upside down in a submissive posture, with the victorious, ventromedially lesioned animal on top of it, sleeping with mouth open and incisors showing. The hyperirritability of the ventromedially lesioned animal does not disappear after a few days, as in the case of the septally lesioned animal, but remains for as long as 2 months.

Similar behavioral changes were reported in a young woman who developed a tumor in the ventromedial hypothalamic region.[45] The great similarity in symptoms makes it clear that the ventromedial hypothalamus did not alter its function very much as the CNS evolved from rodents to man. She first came to the hospital complaining of headaches, excessive thirst and hunger, excessive urination, and a cessation of menstruation. A brain tumor was suspected, but it could not be demonstrated by neurological tests. Two years later the patient was brought back to the hospital. She had doubled her body weight (see Figure 8–2). Her behavior had also changed—she had become withdrawn and was given to frequent outbursts of laughing, crying, and rage. She had had hallucinations and was frequently confused about time and space. During her stay in the hospital she became unmanageable and frequently attacked the nurses and doctors. Her attacks were intense: she tried to kick, punch, and bite. Then she died. An autopsy revealed a tumor restricted to the ventromedial hypothalamic region.

There have been several attempts to parallel the finickiness of the ventromedially lesioned obese animal with the behavior of the obese person. Although ventromedial hypothalamic lesions result in hyperphagia by altering primary regulatory systems, some believe that ventromedial hypothalamic lesions alter the reactivity of an animal to taste stimuli,[25, 57] suggesting that the animal's overeating may simply be a consequence of the kind of

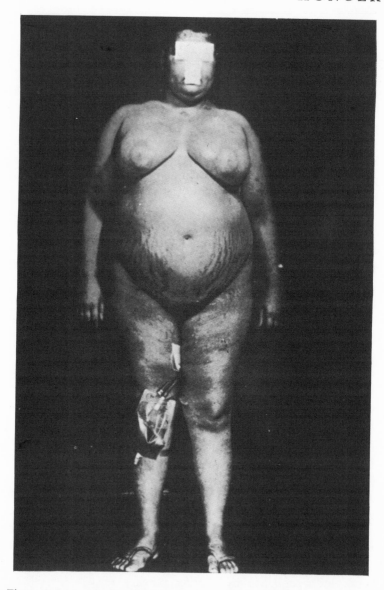

Figure 8–2. A woman afflicted with a tumor of the ventromedial hypothalamus that resulted in overeating and obesity. From A. G. Reeves and
F. Plum. *Arch. Neurol.* 20 (1969): 616. Copyright 1969, American Medical Association. Used with permission of the AMA and A. G. Reeves.

food it is offered. This would also suggest that the ventromedial hypothalamic obese animal is paying more attention to external rather than to internal cues. Lesioned animals, for example, become hyperphagic if they have access to palatable food, but do not if the food is made unpalatable with quinine or is given in a less desirable, dried and powdered form. Ventromedially lesioned animals may thus not really be as motivated to eat as are normal animals.

The obese subject's caloric regulation is more sensitive to, and more easily affected by, external sensory factors than to internal feedback mechanisms. It seems that the obese human, like the obese ventromedially lesioned rat, is also more sensitive to the taste properties of food.[49] Lean persons maintain their normal eating behavior in spite of the adulteration of a food's taste; obese subjects do not. Their caloric intake will decrease, and they may lose weight, if the diet given to them is unpalatable. On the other hand, obese subjects, either rat or human, increase their caloric intake if the food is made more palatable.

The dependency of the obese on environmental cues is illustrated in another experiment.[41] Subjects were invited to participate in an experiment not related to feeding and, while waiting, were individually seated in a room with a table, a chair, and a refrigerator. Since "it happened to be lunch time," a dish holding either 1 or 3 roast beef sandwiches was placed in the middle of the table. Each subject was told that he should feel free to eat, and that there were more sandwiches in the refrigerator to which he could help himself if he finished those on the table. (There actually were more sandwiches in the refrigerator.) Nonobese persons ate approximately 2 sandwiches, whether 1 or 3 sandwiches were placed on the table. Obese persons ate more sandwiches if 3 were placed on the table than if only 1 was placed on it. This provides evidence for a dependency on environmental cues, as well as for a decrease in the motivation to work for food. The presence of only 1 sandwich induces eating, but once it has been consumed, the visual stimulus disappears and eating behavior is turned off. When 3 sandwiches are present, the obese person eats until he has removed the food stimuli from the dish. On the other hand, a lean person maintains his normal caloric intake regardless of the presence or absence of external cues. If 2 sandwiches are his normal lunch, he consumes them, whether they are on the dish or in the refrigerator.

The dependency of obese people on visual cues is also seen when they must lift a weight a number of times to get a bite of food.[28] When they are allowed to see their food through a plastic partition, they respond more times than do lean persons. If they are given a bite of sandwich just prior to the test, they work even harder. Lean persons do not alter the total number of responses in either case. When no food cues are present, obese subjects work even less than do lean persons. In another experiment,[49] obese and lean subjects were confronted with a dish of nuts. In one situation the nuts had a hard shell; in a second situation they had been shelled. Fifty percent of the lean subjects ate the nuts regardless of whether they had to shell them, while 95 percent of the obese subjects ate the nuts when they were already shelled; only 5 percent ate them when they had to shell them themselves.

The results of these experiments, in both animals and man, are not yet fully explained. Animals with lesions of the ventromedial hypothalamus have been shown to work for food at requirements far higher than those already described. They also tolerate food adulteration quite well. Their rejection of dry, powdered food may be a consequence of deficiencies in salivation brought about by disruption of the nerve supply to the salivary glands during surgery, or by the disruption of some salivary function of the ventromedial nucleus itself.[14] Thus, the food rejection may not be related to finickiness. On the other hand, obese persons in their natural environment put in a lot of work to acquire food or to prevent lack of it. Observations made under restrictive experimental conditions do not seem fully in agreement with the long-term effort made by obese persons to maintain their weight and eating habits.

There seems to be no doubt, however, that obese people react differently to environmental stimuli than do lean persons. The reactions of a group of high school students toward the construction of a sanitary landfill next to their town were measured by asking them to classify the favorableness of several statements, with some of the statements relating to olfactory stimuli.[53] The students were classified by weight into very thin, lean, and obese. It was found that obese subjects rated the statements related to odor more objectionable than did the lean and thin subjects, although there was no differentiation among the obese, lean, and thin subjects in their evaluation of statements unrelated to odor. The observed finickiness of obese subjects in the presence of food stimuli apparently can be generalized to odor-related statements as well as to smell. It seems that obese people respond to an odor-related situation by calling upon an attitude structure influenced not only by previous social experience, but also by neurophysiological factors associated with obesity.

TREATMENT OF OBESITY. The only way to lose weight is to create a negative energy balance. This can be achieved by increasing physical activity, by decreasing caloric intake, or both.

When performed methodically, physical exercise helps to reduce weight. In a series of studies,[12] obese persons were assigned to 1 of 2 groups. One group underwent caloric restriction without exercising; the second group exercised as well as dieted. Every person in the second group lost more weight than those who only dieted.

Caloric restriction has long been known as the most efficient treatment for obesity. During the past 50 years many types of diets have been proposed, each claiming to be better than the others. The mere fact that we are still creating new ways of dieting is testimony to the effectiveness and success of our treatment of obesity. In general, weight-reducing diets can be classified in terms of their constituents (e.g., high in protein, high in fats, high in carbohydrates) or in terms of their severeness of caloric restriction (e.g., fasting for a long time, fasting for a short time, or restricted food intake). For the most part, weight loss is independent of the constitution of the diet.[35] That is, a person can lose as much weight by dieting on a carbohydrate-rich, protein-low diet containing 1,000 Kcal. as by dieting on a protein-rich, carbohydrate-low diet containing the same number of calories. Unfortunately, conclusions about the effectiveness of many diets have been reached after short-term studies (1 to 3 weeks). Long-term studies have shown that during the initial period of dieting water is retained in a different way than normal, thus distorting the true weight loss curve. Since the initial weight differences disappear in 3 to 4 weeks, and are due to differences in water retention rather than to loss of fat, conclusions from short-term studies are seldom warranted.

Caloric restriction can be partial or total, and it can be administered for different lengths of time.[6,20] There is no general agreement as to which is the most effective and long-lasting method. Drastic restriction of caloric intake is recommended when the obese person needs prompt reassurance that he can lose weight. Sometimes the health of an individual does not permit rapid weight loss, and a mild caloric restriction is the diet of choice. When the desired body weight has been attained, efforts should be concentrated on keeping it at that level.

BIBLIOGRAPHY

1. Allison, R. B.; Rodriguez, F. L.; Higgins, E. A.; Leddy, J. P.; Abelmann, W. H.; Ellis, L. B.; and Robbins, S. L. Clinicophathologic correlations in coronary atherosclerosis. *Circulation* 27 (1963): 170–184.

2. Angel, J. L. Constitution in female obesity. *Amer. J. Phys. Anthropol.* 7 (1949): 433–471.

3. Bastrup-Madsen, P., and Greisen, O. Hypothalamic obesity in acute leukemia. *Acta Haemat.* 29 (1963): 109–116.

4. Berblinger, K. W. Obesity and psychologic stress. In *Obesity,* ed. N. L. Wilson, pp. 153–160. Philadelphia: F. A. Davis, 1969.

5. Beumont, P. J. Anorexia nervosa: a review. *S. Afr. Med. J.* 44 (1970): 911–916.

6. Bloom, W. L. Fasting as an introduction to the treatment of obesity. *Metabolism* 8 (1959): 214–220.

7. Bolvin, A.; Vendrely, R.; and Vendrely, C. L'acide desoxyribonucleique du noyan cellulaire, depositaire des caracteres hereditaires; arguments d'ordre analytique. *C. R. Acad. Sci.* 226 (1948): 1061.

8. Brainerd, H.; Margen, S.; and Chatton, M. J. *Current diagnosis and treatment.* California: Lange Medical Publications, 1963.

9. Brobeck, J. R.; Tepperman, J.; and Long, C. N. H. Effect of experimental obesity upon carbohydrate metabolism. *Yale J. Biol. Med.* 15 (1943): 893–904.

10. Brown, R. E. Decreased brain weight in malnutrition and its implications. *E. Afr. Med. J.* 11 (1965): 584.

11. Bullen, B. A.; Reed, R. B.; and Mayer, J. Physical activity of obese and nonobese adolescent girls appraised by motion picture sampling. *Amer. J. Clin. Nutr.* 14 (1964): 211–223.

12. Buskirk, E. R. Energy balance of obese patients during weight reduction: influence of diet restriction and exercise. *Ann. N. Y. Acad. Sci.* 110 (1963): 918–940.

13. Cabak, V., and Najdanvic, R. Effect of undernutrition in early life on physical and mental development. *Arch. Dis. Childhood* 40 (1965): 532–534.

14. Coscina, D. V. Behavioral analysis of "dry mouth" in rats following medial hypothalamic lesions. Ph.D. dissertation, Univ. of Chicago, 1971.

15. Cravioto, J. Application of newer knowledge of nutrition on physical and mental growth and development. *Amer. J. Public Health* 53 (1963): 1803–1809.

16. ———. Influencia de la desnutrición en la capacidad de aprendizaje del niño escolar. *Bol. Med. Hosp. Infantil (Mexico)* 24 (1967): 217.

17. ———. Protein metabolism in chronic infantile malnutrition (kwashiorkor), *Amer. J. Clin. Nutr.* 6 (1958): 495–503.

18. ———, and Robles, B. Evolution of adaptive and motor behavior during rehabilitation from kwashiorkor. *Amer. J. Orthopsychiat.* 35 (1965): 449–464.

19. Cravioto, J.; Delicardie, E. R.; and Birch, H. G. Nutrition, growth, and neurointegrative development: an experimental and ecologic study. *Pediatrics* (Suppl. II) 38 (1966): 319–320.

20. Drenick, E. J.; Swendseid, M. E.; Blahd, W. H.; and Tuhle, S. G. Prolonged starvation as a treatment for severe obesity. *J.A.M.A.* 187 (1964): 100–105.

21. Enesco, M., and Leblond, C. P. Increase in cell number as a factor in the growth of the organs of the young male rat. *J. Embryol. Exptl. Morphol.* 10 (1962): 530–562.

22. Fish, I., and Wynick, M. Effect of malnutrition on regional growth of the developing rat brain. *Exptl. Neurol.* 25 (1969): 534–540.

23. Goodsitt, A. Anorexia nervosa. *Brit. J. Med. Psychol.* 42 (1969): 109–118.

24. Gopalan, C., and Srikantia, S. G. Leucine and pellagra. *Lancet* 1 (1960): 954–957.

25. Grossman, S. P. The VMH: a center for affective reactions, satiety, or both? *Physiol. and Behav.* 1 (1966): 1–10.

26. Hirsch, J., and Han, P. W. Cellularity of rat adipose tissue: effects of growth, starvation and obesity. *J. Lipid Res.* 10 (1969): 77–82.

27. Hirsch, J.; Knittle, J. L.; and Salans, L. B. Cell lipid content and cell number in obese and nonobese human adipose tissue. *J. Clin. Invest.* 45 (1966): 1023.

28. Johnson, W. G. The effect of prior-taste and food visibility on the food-directed instrumental performance of obese individuals. Ph.D. dissertation, Catholic Univ. of America, 1970.

29. Kannel, W. B.; LeBauer, E. J.; Dawber, T. R.; and McNamara,

P. M. Relations of body weight to development of coronary heart disease: the Framingham study. *Circulation* 35 (1967): 734–744.

30. Karam, J. H.; Grodsky, G. M.; and Forsham, P. H. The relationship of obesity and growth hormone to serum insulin levels. *Ann. N. Y. Acad. Sci.* 131 (1965): 374–385.

31. Karrer, R., and Cahilly, G. Experimental attempts to produce phenylketonuria in animals: a critical review. *Psychol. Bull.* 64 (1965): 52–64.

32. Kennedy, G. C. The development with age of hypothalamic restraint upon the appetite of the rat. *J. Endocrinol.* 16 (1957): 9–17.

33. Keys, A., and Fidanza, F. Serum cholesterol and relative body weight of coronary patients in different populations. *Circulation* 22 (1960): 1091–1106.

34. King, F. A. Effects of septal and amygdaloid lesions on emotional behavior and conditioned avoidance responses in the rat. *J. Nerv. Ment. Dis.* 126 (1958): 57–63.

35. Kinsell, L. W.; Gunning, B.; Michaels, G. D.; Richardson, J.; Cox, S. E.; and Lemon, C. Calories do count. *Metabolism* 13 (1964): 195–204.

36. Koch, C. R., and Stunkard, A. J. Obesity, age, and gastric hunger contractions. *J. Appl. Physiol.* 15 (1960): 133–134.

37. Kugelmass, I. N.; Poull, L. E.; and Samuel, E. L. Nutritional improvement of child mentality. *Amer. J. Med. Sci.* 208 (1944): 631–633.

38. Mayer, J. Some aspects of the problem of regulation of food intake and obesity. *New England J. Med.* 274 (1966): 662–673.

39. ———; Bates, M. W.; and Dickie, M. M. Hereditary diabetes in genetically obese mice. *Science* 113 (1951): 746–747.

40. McCance, R. A., and Widdowson, E. M. Nutrition and growth. *Proc. Roy. Soc. (London), B* 156 (1962): 326.

41. Nisbett, R. E. Determinants of food intake in obesity. *Science* 159 (1968): 1254–1255.

42. ———, and Gurwitz, S. B. Weight, sex, and the eating behavior of human newborns. *J. Comp. Physiol. Psychol.* 73 (1970): 245–253.

43. Peckham, S. C.; Entenman, C.; and Carroll, H. W. The influence of a hypercaloric diet on gross body and adipose tissue composition in the rat. *J. Nutrition* 77 (1962): 187–197.

44. Politzer, W. M., and Bersohn, I. Biochemical changes resulting from drastic weight loss in obesity. *S. Afr. Med. J.* 37 (1963): 151–154.

45. Reeves, A. G., and Plum, F. Hyperphagia, rage, and dementia accompanying a ventromedial hypothalamic neoplasm. *Arch. Neurol.* 20 (1969): 616–624.

46. Ross, M. H. Length of life and nutrition in the rat. *J. Nutrition* 75 (1961): 197–210.

47. ———. Nutrition, disease and length of life. In *Diet and bodily constitution,* ed. G. E. W. Wolstenholme and M. O'Connor, pp. 90–103. Boston: Little, Brown, 1964.

48. Russell, O. F. Metabolic, endocrine and psychiatric aspects of anorexia nervosa. *Sci. Basis Med. Ann. Rev.* (1969): 236–255.

49. Schachter, S. Some extraordinary facts about obese humans and rats. *Amer. Psychol.* 26 (1971): 129–144.

50. Spies, T. D.; Aring, C. D.; Gelpernin, J.; and Bean, W. B. The mental symptoms of pellagra. Their relief with nicotinic acid. *Amer. J. Med. Sci.* 196 (1938): 461–475.

51. Stoch, M. B., and Smythe, P. M. Does undernutrition during infancy inhibit brain growth and subsequent intellectual development? *Arch. Dis. Childhood* 38 (1963): 546–552.

52. Strang, J. M. Obesity. In *Diseases of metabolism. Detailed methods of diagnosis and treatment* 4th ed., ed. G. G. Duncan. Philadelphia: W. B. Saunders, 1959.

53. Strodtbeck, F. L.; Madsen, B.; and Balagura, S. Olfactory attitude consistency and obesity. Unpublished manuscript, 1971.

54. Stunkard, A. J. Eating patterns and obesity. *Psychiat. Quart.* 33 (1959): 284–295.

55. ———. Obesity. In *Encyclopedia of mental health,* ed. A. Deutsch, vol. 4, p. 1372. New York: Franklin Watts, 1963.

56. ———, and Mendelson, M. Disturbances in body image of some obese persons. *J. Amer. Diet. Assn.,* 38 (1961): 328–331.

57. Teitelbaum, P. Sensory control of hypothalamic hyperphagia. *J. Comp. Physiol. Psychol.* 48 (1955): 156–163.

58. Westall, R. G.; Roitman, E.; de la Peña, C.; Rasmussen, H.; Cravioto, J.; Gomez, F.; and Holt, L. E. The plasma amino acids in malnutrition: preliminary observations. *Arch. Dis. Child* 33 (1958): 499–504.

59. Widdowson, E. M., and McCance, R. A. The effect of finite periods of undernutrition at different ages on the composition and subsequent development of the rat. *Proc. Roy. Soc. (London),* B 158 (1963): 329–342.

60. ———. Some effects of accelerating growth. I. General somatic development. *Proc. Roy. Soc. (London),* B 152 (1960): 188–206.

61. Wilson, N. L.; Farber, S. M.; Kimbrough, L. D.; and Wilson, R. H. L. The development and perpetuation of obesity: an overview. In *Obesity,* ed. Nancy L. Wilson, pp. 3–12. Philadelphia: F. A. Davis, 1969.

62. Winick, M. Changes in nucleic acid and protein content of the human brain during growth. *Pediat. Res.* 2 (1968): 352–355.

63. ———. Fetal malnutrition and growth processes. *Hosp. Pract.* 5 (1970): 33–41.

64. ———, and Noble, A. Cellular response in rat during malnutrition at various ages. *J. Nutrition* 89 (1966): 300–306.

65. ———. Cellular response with increased feeding in neonatal rats. *J. Nutrition* 91 (1967): 179–182.

66. ———. Quantitative changes in DNA, RNA and protein during prenatal and postnatal growth in the rat. *Dev. Biol.* 12 (1965): 451–466.

67. Winick, M., and Rosso, P. Effects of severe early malnutrition on cellular growth of human brain. *Pediat. Res.* 3 (1969): 181–184.

68. ———. Head circumference and cellular growth of the brain in normal and marasmic children. *J. Pediatrics* 74 (1969): 774–778.

69. Wohl, M. G. Obesity. In *Modern nutrition in health and disease,* ed. M. G. Wohl and R. S. Goodhart, pp. 971–989. Philadelphia: Lea & Febiger, 1968.

70. Yalow, R. S.; Glick, S. M.; Roth, J.; and Berson, S. A. Plasma insulin and growth hormone levels in obesity and diabetes. *Ann. N. Y. Acad. Sci.* 131 (1965): 357–373.

SUGGESTED SUPPLEMENTARY READINGS

Burgess, A., and Dean, R. F. A. eds. *Malnutrition and food habits.* New York: Macmillan, 1962.

Coursin, D. B. Nutrition and brain function. In *Modern nutrition in health and disease,* ed. M. G. Wohl and R. S. Goodhart, pp. 1070–1085. Philadelphia: Lea and Febiger, 1968.

Eichenwald, H. F., and Fry, P. C. Nutrition and learning. *Science* 163 (1969): 644–648.

Kaufman, M. R. ed. *Anorexia nervosa.* New York: International Universities Press, 1964.

Mayer, J., *Overweight: causes, cost, and control.* Englewood Cliffs, N. J.: Prentice Hall, 1968.

Index

Index

(septum), 21, 71, 72; of sheep, 135; and specific hungers, 133–148; stimulus-bound, 46, 47; and striatum, 30; suppression of, 46; and taste, 30, 105, 114, 116; and temporal lobes, 66, 67; and 2DG, 92; and ventromedial hypothalamus, 20–21, 31, 46, 48, 54–56; of Wisconsin timber wolves, 14. *See also* Anorexia; Aphagia; Food intake; Hyperphagia; Malnutrition; Obesity
Energy, 3, 4, 5, 18, 34, 85
Energy regulation, 28, 78–96
Energy reserves, 4, 34, 85
Enterogastrone, 39, 121, 124
Entorhinal cortex, 66, 70, 72, 73
Enzymes, 36, 39
Epinephrine, 89, 90
Erdheim, J., 45
Esophagus, 28, 36
Experimental Investigations of the Functions of the Nervous System in Vertebrates (Flourenz), 41
Extrapyramidal area, 65

Facial nerve, 108
Fasting, 88, 119, 120, 161
Fat (adipose) cells, 85, 160, 162, 163
Fat deposits, 4, 83, 84, 85, 88
Fats (lipids), 5, 39, 59, 87, 94, 134
Fatty acids, 84, 88
Feeding behavior, *see* Eating (feeding) behavior; Periodic eating behavior
Feeding system, 7, 8, 74
Finickiness, 56–57, 71
Flourenz, Pierre, 41
Food deprivation, 119, 120
Food intake: and amino acids, 86, 138, 139; and aminostatic theory, 86; and amygdala, 67, 68, 69; and anterior hypothalamus, 95; and autonomic nervous system, 28; and body temperature regulation, 93; and calories, 122, 123–124, 141; and carbohydrates, 139, 141; and central nervous system damage, 65; and chewing, 110–111; and diet deficiencies, 138,

139, 140, 141; and enterogastrone, 39; and environmental temperature, 94; extrahypothalamic mechanisms of, 67; and glucagon, 89, 93; and glucose, 93; glucostatic theory of, 87; and hippocampus, 70; and humorstatic theory, 81, 82; and hypothalamus, 41, 45; increase in, 45, 46; and insulin, 88, 89, 93, 139, 141; and intestinal distention, 122–123; and lateral hypothalamus, 49–50; lipostatic theory of, 83–85; and neural transmission, 95; and nutritional value, 115, 117; oropharyngeal factors, 110; and palatability, 116; and parabiosis, 81, 82; and preoptic area, 95; and pyriform cortex, 67, 73; regulation of, 28, 86; and septal area (septum), 71; and sodium, 134, 142–144; and specific dynamic action (SDA), 94; and specific needs, 138, 139; and stomach distention, 122; and swallowing, 110–111; and taste, 116–118; and temporal lobes, 66; and thalamus, 72; and thermostatic theory of, 93, 94; and thiamin (vitamin B$_1$) deficiency, 144; and ventromedial hypothalamus, 46; and vitamin B-complex, 139. *See also* Anorexia; Aphagia; Hyperphagia; Malnutrition; Obesity
Foodstuffs, 4, 5, 6, 14, 94, 114, 115, 135–148
Forebrain, 29. *See also* Diencephalon; Telencephalon
Frontal lobes, 21, 29, 73
Frontotemporal cortex, 66
Fructose, 141

Gagging, 68
Gall bladder, 39
Gastric contractions, *see* Gastric motility; Stomach (gastric) contractions
Gastric motility, 20, 89, 120, 121, 122, 126. *See also* Stomach (gastric) contractions
Gastric secretions, 28, 89

Index

Larynx, 108
Lashley's equipotentiality hypothesis, 50–51
Lateral hypothalamus, 21, 31, 46, 47, 48, 49, 50, 51, 53, 54, 56, 57, 58, 68, 73, 82, 90, 92, 120
Laurence-Moon-Biedl syndrome, 162
Le Magnen, J., 11, 13
Lesioning, 43–44
Leucine, 157
Licking, 6, 68, 73
Liebelt, R. A., 84
Limbic cortices, 65, 72–73
Limbic system, 30, 65, 71, 107–108
Lipase, 39
Lipostatic theory of energy regulation, 78, 83–85, 91
Liver, 28, 29, 39, 88, 90, 91, 161, 162
Liver glucogenolysis, 28
Locomotor activity, 14, 15, 19, 20
Luckhardt, A. B., and Carlson, A. J., 79
Lysencephalic cortex, 29

MacLean, P. D., and Delgado, J. M. R., 68
Malnutrition: anorexia nervosa, 159–160; and brain damage, 152; and growth, 155, 156; and mental retardation, 156, 158; and pregnancy, 157, 158; and proportion of nutrients in diet, 134
Maltase, 39
Mammillary bodies, 31
Mastication, see Chewing
Mayer, J., 87
Meal length, 9, 15
Meals, 9, 11, 12, 13, 14, 15
Meal size, 9, 14, 15, 55, 124
Medulla oblongata, 29
Mellinkoff, S. M., 86
Mesencephalon, 29. See also Midbrain
Metabolic pools, 18
Metabolic substrates, 34
Metabolization, 5
Midbrain, 29, 30, 32, 34, 74, 109
Midbrain reticular formation, 33, 74
Mohr, B., 45
Molar response, 18

Mongolism, 157
Mouth, 36. See also Oropharyngeal eating system
Müller, J., 106
Multicellular organisms, 18

Neocortex, 29
Nervous system, 25–34, 42, 43. See also Autonomic nervous system (ANS); Central nervous system (CNS)
Neuroendocrine system, 18
Neurohumoral theory of energy regulation, 78, 95–96
Niacin, 139, 157
Norepinephrine, 69, 70, 72, 73, 95
Nutrition: and brain growth, 153, 155; and food intake, 115, 117. See also Malnutrition

Obesity: and adipose (fat) cells, 160, 162, 163; and anxiety, 163; and boredom, 164; and brain lesions, 163; and brain tumors, 45, 163; and caloric restriction, 169; and cardiovascular disease, 162; causes of, 160, 162–164; and cholesterol, 162; consequences of, 160–162; cultural influences and, 163; and decreased activity, 164; and defense mechanisms, 163; and depression, 163; and diabetes mellitus, 161, 162; and displacement activities, 163; and eating behavior, 83; and endocrine imbalance, 162; and entorhinal cortex, 73; and environmental cues, 167–169; environmentally caused, 85; and exercise, 169; and external sensory factors, 167; and fasting, 161; and fat cell increase, 85, 162, 163; genetically caused, 162; and glucose 161; and GTG, 91; and humorstatic theory, 81; and hyperglycemia, 161; and hypothalamus, 45; Laurence-Moon-Biedl syndrome, 162; and life span, 161; and lipostatic theory, 83, 84, 85; and liver, 161; medical management of, 85; and metabolic changes, 45, 46; and olfactory stimuli, 169; and para-

Obesity (*cont.*)
biosis, 18; and pituitary gland, 45; as positive energy balance, 4, 160; and proportion of nutrients in diet, 134; psychological consequences of, 160; psychological management of, 85; and severe neurosis, 164; and taste, 167; treatment of, 169–170; and ventromedial hypothalamus, 45, 160. *See also* Hyperphagia
Occipital lobe, 29
Odor stimuli, 106
Olds, J., 58
Olfaction (smell), 30, 66, 73, 105, 106, 107, 108, 113
Olfactory bulbs, 107, 108
Olfactory complex, 66
Olfactory system, 107–108
Oropharyngeal eating system, 109–118
Osmoreceptor system, 125
Osmotic effects, 124–125

Palatability, 116. *See also* Taste
Paleocortex, 29
Pancreas, 39, 87
Pancreozymin, 39
Papez, J. W., 66, 67
Parabiosis, 79–82
Parasympathetic nervous system, 27, 28, 40
Parietal lobe, 29
Pellagra, 157
Peptidases, 39
Periodic behavior, 9–10, 18–21
Periodic eating behavior, 7, 11–12, 13, 14–17, 19, 20, 21
Peripheral nervous system, 27
Peristalsis, 28, 36, 40
Pharynx, 28, 36, 108
Phenylalanine, 157
Phenylketonuria, 157
Phospholipids, 156
Pineal body, 21, 32
Pituitary gland (hypophysis), 45, 59
Pons, 29
Posterior hypothalamus, 120
Postganglionic neurons, 28
Predation and ingestion, 6
Preganglionic neurons, 28

Preoptic area, 94, 95
Prepyriform complex, 66
Proteins, 5, 21, 38–39, 86, 87, 94, 134, 138, 139, 152, 156. *See also* Amino acids
Ptyalin, 36
Pyloric sphincter, 39
Pyriform cortex, 67, 72, 73

Rectum, 28, 40
Red nuclei, 34
Respiration, 3
Rhinencephalon, 66
Riboflavin, 139
Richter, C. P., 9–10, 12, 19, 20, 21
Richter, C. P., and Eckert, J. F., 143

Salivary glands, 28, 36
Salivary nuclei, 36
Salivation, 28, 36, 73, 94, 168
Satiety: and amygdala, 69; and calories, 122, 123–124; and carbohydrates, 94; and chewing, 109, 110; and enterogastrone, 39, 124; and fats (lipids), 94; and fatty acids in blood, 84; and gastrointestinal system, 118–126; and glucostatic theory, 90; and humorstatic theory, 82; and intestinal distention, 122–123, 124; and lateral hypothalamus, 48–49, 90; and osmotic pressure, 124–125; and protein, 94; and self-stimulation, 58; and stomach, 111–113; and stomach distention, 122, 124; and swallowing, 109, 110; and 2DG, 92; and ventromedial hypothalamus, 48–49, 90
Secretin, 39
Septal area (septum), 21, 65, 66, 71, 72, 164
Small intestine, 38–40
Smell, *see* Olfaction (smell)
Sniffing, 68, 72
Sodium, 134, 142–144, 146
Solitary tract, 109
Somatic nervous system, 27
Somatomotor actions, 27
Specific dynamic action (SDA) of food, 94

Index

Specific hungers: and amino acid regulation of food intake, 86; definition, 133; and diet deficiencies, 138–145; and eating behavior, 133; genetic theory of, 145–147, 148; in humans, 133–134; learned, 145, 146, 147, 148; and self-selection, 134–138
Spinal nerves, 27
Splanchnic nerve, 125
Starches, 36
Starvation, 48, 79
Stereotaxic instrument, 42
Stimulation procedures, 43, 44
Stomach: acidity of, 28, 125; and autonomic nervous system, 28; corpus region, 36; digestive juices, 37–38; distention of, 122–123, 125; and drinking behavior, 110; emptying rate of, 125; and food, 36, 38; and food intake, 122; and hunger, 119, 122; "hunger contractions" of, 19, 20; hydrochloric acid in, 37; and locomotor activity, 19; mixing movements of, 38; motility of, 28; necessity of, 122; osmoreceptors of, 125; pepsin in, 37; and periodic behavior, 20; and periodic eating behavior, 19; removal of, 122; and satiety, 111–113, 118, 122–123, 124, 126; sensory mechanisms of, 125; and splanchnic nerve, 125; and sympathetic nervous system, 28; and taste, 117–118; and vagus nerve, 28, 36, 125
Stomach (gastric) contractions, 19, 20, 86–87, 88, 119, 120, 121. *See also* Gastric motility
Stria medullaris, 72
Striatum, 30, 74
Strumwasser, F., 21
Subcallosal cortex, 66
Substantia nigra, 33, 74
Sucrase, 39

Sulci, 29
Swallowing, 9, 36, 73, 109, 110, 111
Swann, H., 108
Sympathetic nervous system, 27, 28

Taste, 30, 50, 56, 57, 105, 106, 107, 108, 109, 110, 113, 115, 116, 117, 118
Taste stimuli, 105
Telencephalon, 29, 30, 74
Temporal lobes, 29, 65, 66, 67
Thalamus, 66, 72, 109
Thermostatic theory of energy regulation, 78, 93–95
Thiamin hydrochloride (vitamin B_1), 139, 144, 145
Tongue, 106, 108
Triglycerides, 88
Trypsin, 39
Tryptophane, 157
2-deoxy-D-glucose (2DG), 91–92
Tyrosine, 157

Undernourishment, 4. *See also* Malnutrition
Unicellular animals, 5, 18

Vacuoles, 5
Vagus nerve, 28, 29, 36, 39, 88, 90, 108, 120, 121, 125
Ventral tegmentum, 74
Ventromedial hypothalamus, 20–21, 31, 45, 46, 47, 48, 51, 53, 54, 55, 56, 57, 67, 68, 69, 71, 72, 81, 83, 84, 89, 90, 91, 92, 95, 120, 164, 165, 167, 168
Villi, 40
Visceromotor responses, 27
Viscerosensory stimuli, 27
Vitamin B-complex, 139, 145, 147. *See also* Niacin; Thiamin hydrochloride (vitamin B_1)
Vitamin B_1, *see* Thiamin hydrochloride (vitamin B_1)
Vitamins, 157